D0124548

DALE EARNHARDT, JR.

Racing's Living Legacy

by James MacDonald

Enslow Publishers, Inc.
40 Industrial Road
Box 398
Berkeley Heights, NJ 07922
USA
http://www.enslow.com

Library of Congress Cataloging-in-Publication Data
MacDonald, James (James Gregory), 1971-
  Dale Earnhardt, Jr. : racing's living legacy / James MacDonald.
     p. cm. — (Heroes of racing)
  Summary: "A biography of NASCAR sports star Dale Earnhardt, Jr"—Provided by publisher.
  Includes bibliographical references and index.
  ISBN-13: 978-0-7660-2996-5
  ISBN-10: 0-7660-2996-4
 1. Earnhardt, Dale, Jr.—Juvenile literature. 2. Stock car drivers—United States—Biography—Juvenile literature. I. Title.
  GV1032.E19M33 2008
  796.72'092—dc22
  [B]
                                            2007016054

Credits
Editorial Direction: Red Line Editorial (Bob Temple)
Editor: Sue Green
Designer: Becky Daum

Printed in the United States of America

10 9 8 7 6 5 4 3 2

To Our Readers: We have done our best to make sure all Internet addresses in this book were active and appropriate when we went to press. However, the author and the publisher have no control over and assume no liability for the material available on those Internet sites or on other Web sites they may link to. Any comments or suggestions can be sent by e-mail to comments@enslow.com or to the address on the back cover.

Disclaimer: This publication is not affiliated with, endorsed by, or sponsored by NASCAR. NASCAR®, WINSTON CUP®, NEXTEL CUP, BUSCH SERIES and CRAFTSMAN TRUCK SERIES are trademarks owned or controlled by the National Association for Stock Car Auto Racing, Inc., and are registered where indicated.

Photo credits: Mike McCarn/AP Images, 1; Terry Renna/AP Images, 4, 28, 94; Phil Coale/AP Images, 9, 55; Gerry Broome/AP Images, 15, 76; Harold Hinson/AP Images, 21; Dale Atkins/AP Images, 33; Albuquerque Journal, Greg Sorber/AP Images, 38; David Taylor/Getty Images, 44; Chuck Burton/AP Images, 51; Chris O'Meara/AP Images, 53, 74; Ric Feld/AP Images, 63; Mary Ann Chastain/AP Images, 66; Peter Cosgrove/AP Images, 68; Reinhold Matay/AP Images, 71; Wilfredo Lee/AP Images, 79; The Charlotte Observer, Erik Perel/AP Images, 84; Luis Alvarez/AP Images, 97; Jim Cole/AP Images, 98; Rainier Ehrdardt/AP Images, 103; Chuck Burton/AP Images, 105; LM Otero/AP Images, 110; The Charlotte Observer, Jeff Siner/AP Images, 113

Cover Photo: Mike McCarn/AP Images

CONTENTS

THE WORST TURN

It was to have been his coming out party. Many experts had predicted it. In a bold and brazen flash, even he had predicted it.

Dale Earnhardt, Jr. would win the 2001 Daytona 500.

Though he was only twenty-six years old, Earnhardt, Jr. dreamed of taking the checkered flag in only his second try at the biggest jewel in NASCAR's crown. The son of NASCAR legend Dale Earnhardt, Sr. turned that dream into a prediction.

"Out front all day," he said.[1]

Dale Earnhardt, Jr. takes a break in the garage during practice at Daytona International Speedway.

He meant hardly anyone would challenge him for 500 miles. The revealing vision was full of hope. It also showed a hint of the swagger that seemed to come so naturally to him.

That day, Earnhardt, Jr. was on the verge of becoming NASCAR's future and present at the same time. He had the chance to show the world why he was the most popular driver in the most popular new sport in the country.

Sadly, that day became tragic.

OPENING DAY

It was February 18, 2001, and the NASCAR season was about to begin as it always does—with the Daytona 500. Held in Daytona Beach, Florida, the Daytona 500 is also known as the "Great American Race."

Almost three months had passed since the end of the 2000 season. The famous 2.5-mile track again became the center of the racing world.

The Daytona 500 boasts a proud history. Each year, it ranks as the most anticipated race on the calendar.

TRACK FACT
The first Daytona 500 took place on February 22, 1959.

The top finisher would make as much money in one day as many people make in their lifetimes. The event is a dazzling display of a sport on the rise.

By the time the race started, nearly 200,000 fans lined the track. Tens of millions more would watch on television. They were ready to cheer for their favorite drivers.

Many cheered loudest for Junior's dad. At 49, Earnhardt, Sr. was an old-school racing hero. He was as tough and strong as the steel of his unmistakably black No. 3 car. Earnhardt, Sr.'s dad, Ralph Earnhardt, was a champion driver in the 1950s. He passed along the honest work ethic that would drive his son.

Earnhardt, Sr. collected more than $40 million on the racetrack. He earned countless fans in the process. Earnhardt, Sr. had won seven NASCAR points championships in twenty-two seasons. He once won eleven races in a season. He was a dynasty.

People owned No. 3 buttons, T-shirts, and hats in all shapes and sizes. They would show them off at races. Earnhardt, Sr.'s work ethic was admired by many, and he was an idol to numerous people.

To racing fans, "Earnhardt" was already a household name. Earnhardt, Jr. was on the verge of becoming as famous as his father.

THE NEXT GENERATION

The same loyal fans who rooted for Earnhardt, Sr. took a liking to his confident young son. Earnhardt,

Jr. also earned his own following. He seemed to have more fans than anyone.

Junior was a new-school star. He played video games. He wore cool sunglasses and turned his hat backward. He listened to hip-hop music and appeared on MTV. He was a little bit country and a little bit rock 'n' roll. While his father had strength, Junior had polish. He was a natural. In other words, he was a perfect fit for the sport.

NASCAR used to be a regional sport. Stars such as Jeff Gordon and Tony Stewart helped make it more famous. They were thought of as a new generation.

Earnhardt, Jr. was literally the next generation. He started to become the face of the sport's future. His father provided a blueprint for how to achieve success in the future. Junior idolized him.

"This man could lead the world's finest army," Junior said of his father in 2000. "He has wisdom that knows no bounds. No fire could burn his character, no stone could break it."[2]

Like most sons, he wanted to earn his father's respect. It was not always easy. His father could be hard on him. Earning respect took time. The effort was worth every minute.

"His friendship is the greatest gift you could ever obtain," Junior said. "Out of all his attributes, it is the most impressive. He trusts only a few with this gift. If you ever break that trust—it is over. He

Dale Earnhardt, Jr. (8) and Dale Earnhardt, Sr. run together near the end of the Daytona 500.

accepts few apologies. Many have crossed him and they leave with only regret for their actions. In every result, he stands as an example of what hard work and dedication will achieve."[3]

The pair became closer as Junior grew older. They began to share their lives as two adults. Junior hit NASCAR's top circuit two years earlier. Earnhardt,

Sr.'s friends noticed a change. The grizzled veteran had a different spirit.

"These past two years, having Junior on the track, we've all seen a marked change in Dale," David Allen said.[4] Allen was Earnhardt, Sr.'s public relations manager. That "marked" change was in Earnhardt, Sr. He was more upbeat now that he was racing alongside his son.

Earnhardt, Sr. was gaining something his son already had. He was gaining a chance to have his life enhanced by the other Dale Earnhardt's personality.

By 2001, they both possessed the ability to win NASCAR's season championship. Earnhardt, Sr. could win as a veteran in his No. 3 car. Earnhardt, Jr. could win as a young man in his No. 8 car. It all started with the Daytona 500.

THE BIG RACE

The forecast called for sunshine and temperatures in the mid-60s. One sportswriter summed it up with a single word: Perfect.

Unfortunately, more than forty drivers had to share the road. They all wanted to win fame and fortune. Weather would be the easiest thing to predict.

Not so easy to predict are the actions of other drivers and the performance of their cars. During NASCAR races, bright and shiny cars dart across blacktop. They growl toward 200 miles per hour (322 kilometers per hour). Drivers swerve in and out of traffic. They are forced to make split-second decisions from steamy and cramped cockpits. No two laps look the same. Not a single second is dull.

But each race starts the same way. Keeping with the tradition, the 2001 season opened with the most familiar words in racing.

"Gentlemen, start your engines!"

Earnhardt, Sr., Earnhardt, Jr., racing team-mate Michael Waltrip, and the others flipped the ignition switches. They gunned the engines. Their 800-horsepower monsters barked out roars from under the hood.

Earnhardt, Sr. was the most decorated driver at Daytona. He started the race seventh in the starting grid. The starting grid was made of two long lanes of traffic. Earnhardt, Sr. was in the fourth row.

Junior was diagonally in front of him in the sixth spot. Waltrip was back in the tenth row. All forty-three cars followed the pace car to the track. Two hundred laps of action followed.

Soon, the field was at full throttle. Cars snaked

TRACK FACT

Dale Earnhardt, Sr. holds the record for most times completing all 500 miles of the Daytona 500. He finished the race fourteen times.

around the track. They banked high together around the corners. Then they would level out in the straightaways. From far away, the cars on the track looked like a colorful pool of liquid swirling around a big tub.

During the course of the race, the lead changed forty-nine times. Waltrip and the Earnhardts each led at least one lap. Around and around the track they went. Tensions mounted with each lap.

Near the end of the race, a chain-reaction crash took out nearly twenty of the cars. Crews cleaned up the damage from the crash. With twenty-five laps remaining at the time of the crash, the restart caused a dash for the finish line.

The green flag waved. The drivers revved their cars to top speed again.

Earnhardt, Jr. and veteran Sterling Marlin traded the lead. Waltrip worked himself into the mix. Soon, three drivers found themselves at the front of the pack. The last few turns approached.

The Man in Black, as Earnhardt, Sr. was known, ran third. Earnhardt, Jr. ran second. In front was Waltrip. He was about to win his first NASCAR race, at the Daytona 500 of all places.

The rush of excitement drew the fans out of their seats. They were witnessing something special. It was one of NASCAR's more thrilling moments. The old veteran was clogging up traffic while shepherding the two cars he owned to Victory Lane. One was driven by his son. The other was commanded by a guy who had not won a single race in his career.

Had the race ended right there, that lap would have made for a wonderful ending to a perfect race day. But six seconds before Waltrip crossed the finish line—barely in front of Earnhardt, Jr.—something terrible had happened. Cars bumped just behind the top two finishers. The familiar black No. 3 was suddenly going the wrong way. After the contact, Earnhardt, Sr.'s car took a quick right turn. It headed toward the outside of the track. It climbed up the hill of the steep banking, and Earnhardt, Sr. hit the wall nearly head-on.

A few hundred yards ahead, his son had finished a very close second in the sport's biggest race. He won $975,907. It did not matter. His father's car had slid back down the track and into the infield.

Dale Earnhardt, Sr.—NASCAR legend, idol, and father—had died.

"I lost the greatest man I ever knew, my dad," Junior said.[5]

CARRYING ON

February 18, 2001, became a tragic day for the Great American Race and NASCAR. It was especially tragic for the legend's son.

Junior found himself in a very sad place. Even though he had won almost $1 million, the worst days of his young life were just ahead. He tried hard to be strong.

Seven days after the tragic incident, Earnhardt, Jr. raced his No. 8 again. It was at NASCAR's next stop in Rockingham, North Carolina. As his autobiography says, he is Driver #8. He drives racecars.

"We'll get through this," he said. "I'm sure he'd want us to keep going, and that's what we're going to do."[6]

The sport the Earnhardts live and love is defined by going around and around, but it is their success through life's ups and downs that best defines them. In Junior's case, through his darkest days, he managed to get back on his feet and back on the track.

His father's lessons about being strong and showing courage were real.

A candle burns in tribute to Dale Earnhardt, Sr.

Looking back, it is no surprise that Earnhardt, Jr. learned strength and courage. And it is no wonder he is his own man as an adult.

His childhood was not ideal. He did not have it as easy as many kids did. Even though his father would become rich and famous, the road to family fortune was a long one. And it was not always smooth.

To follow it requires retracing Earnhardt, Sr.'s steps back to Kannapolis, North Carolina. It is not far from Charlotte—not in miles, anyway.

Born in 1951, Earnhardt, Sr. grew up fast—maybe too fast. He was a teenager when he married his first wife in 1968. The couple had a son named Kerry in 1969. They divorced shortly afterward.

Earnhardt, Sr. then began to date Brenda Gee. He was still quite young.

Brenda came from a racing family. Her father, Robert Gee, is a well-known pioneer in the racing industry. He helped build engines. He also shaped the bodies of racecars.

Earnhardt, Sr. and Brenda married in 1971. On August 28, 1972, they had a daughter and named her Kelley.

CHASING A DREAM

Earnhardt, Sr.'s family was growing. So was his appetite for racing cars. Often, he thought it was the one thing he wanted.

It was his dream to race. His reality was more complicated. He was starting a family. Racing was not a guaranteed future, no matter how much promise he showed. And he did not have a high school diploma.

Still only twenty-two, life dealt Earnhardt, Sr. another blow. In 1973, he lost his father, Ralph.

"It was a heck of a deal," he said in 1998 as he looked back.[1]

Before Earnhardt, Sr. built his racing empire, he struggled. Finding a good job was not easy. He had worked in a nearby factory and at other jobs that were not permanent. He was not working full time. He was, however, falling in debt.

In 1974, another child came. It was a boy.

Born on October 10, 1974, Earnhardt, Jr. was given the name Ralph Dale Earnhardt. He and his father share the name in tribute to Earnhardt, Jr.'s grandfather.

The children of many prominent athletes grow up at their parents' versions of the office. Ballplayers take their kids to the ballpark. Hockey players take their kids to the rink. Some children even grow up to become good at the same sports as their parents with the help of this upbringing.

For Earnhardt, Jr., it was different.

Earnhardt, Sr. was showing potential on the racetrack. His career path was pulling him away. By 1977, when Earnhardt, Jr. was only three years old, Earnhardt, Sr. and Brenda divorced. Earnhardt, Jr. and Kelley would live with their mother. They would not live with their father for another three years. Earnhardt, Sr. went to work on his budding career.

By 1979, Earnhardt, Sr. had become a full-time driver on NASCAR's top circuit. He was not driving the familiar No. 3 car then. He drove the No. 2. The young driver and his car made quite an impact at Earnhardt, Sr.'s first Daytona 500. At one point, he even cruised out to the lead. He finished eighth, but he put many big names behind him. It was a brief moment, but what a moment it was.

GAINING FAME

Earnhardt, Sr.'s next big moment came a few months later.

He won his first race on April 1, 1979. His hard work and dedication had paid off. Who had been in his rearview mirror that day? Bobby Allison, Darrell Waltrip, and "The King," Richard Petty. They were the circuit's legends. Earnhardt, Sr. had beaten them. The win confirmed big things were to come for the young racer.

Earnhardt, Sr. was gaining fame on the national stage, but his own son did not really know him.

"I knew a little bit about my father," Earnhardt, Jr. said of those times, "but not a lot."[2]

Earnhardt, Sr. was named Rookie of the Year in 1979. He also earned $237,575 in winnings. The next year, he nearly doubled that.

In 1980, Earnhardt, Sr. was the circuit's top driver. He won five races and the points championship. He also became the first driver to win a championship one year after being named Rookie of the Year.

Off the track, Earnhardt, Sr. fished, socialized,

DID YOU KNOW? The NASCAR schedule, even in the early 1980s, featured at least thirty races per year.

and visited his children when he could. On the track, he was tough. Sometimes he broke bones during crashes. He bounced back quickly from his injuries. Few drivers were more resilient.

Not quite thirty, he was still younger than many on the track. In those days, racing was a veterans' game. Still, Earnhardt, Sr. turned out to be plenty mature. He also had an appeal.

The New York Times ran a feature on Earnhardt, Sr. in August 1980. Earnhardt, Jr. had not yet turned six years old. In the article, Earnhardt, Sr. said of racing, "It never even occurred to me that I'd be doin' anything else."[3]

Not only was Earnhardt, Sr. a genuine racecar driver, he was now one of the best. He was also a parent. Juggling the two responsibilities proved difficult.

THEY SAID IT

"A lot of my fondest memories were being a little kid and I had my Matchbox cars playing on the carpet while Dad was running the race."

— Dale Earnhardt, Jr.

Kelley Earnhardt sits next to a photo of her brother and father.

The same article talked about "two deliciously sassy and bright children" from his marriage to Brenda.[4] It was talking about Kelley and Earnhardt, Jr.

Life would soon change for them, too.

MOVING IN WITH DAD

While Earnhardt, Sr. chased his dreams, one of Earnhardt, Jr.'s dreams was about to come true. Unfortunately, it came at a high price. With the Earnhardts, it sometimes seems nearly everything happens that way.

In 1981, Earnhardt, Jr. was six years old, and Kelley was eight. A fire tore through their house. Their home was destroyed. Luckily, the family members were all safe. Sadly, Brenda had to move. She would go to Virginia. Her children went to live with their father.

Earnhardt, Jr. had lived with his father only half of his young life. It took a fire wrecking his house and his mother moving away to be reunited with Earnhardt, Sr.

The trying circumstance did something for Earnhardt, Jr. and Kelley. That fire helped the siblings bond. They felt isolated at times. Their relationship became special then. It remains special today. Earnhardt, Jr. and his sister moved near to their father's childhood home in Kannapolis.

Those were bittersweet days for Earnhardt, Jr. He might have been living with his father, but the racecar driver was focused on his career. Earnhardt, Sr. was not always available.

Earnhardt, Jr. and Kelley were often cared for by babysitters or nannies. Kelley became like a second mother to her little brother.

"Dad was there when he could be," Kelley said in July 2006. "But he was still making the kind of sacrifices he had to make to become what he wanted to be."[5]

By 1982, Earnhardt, Sr. made a good living, but that living required thousands of miles in travel. From February to November, he raced thirty Sundays. That meant thirty Sundays away from home.

Earnhardt, Jr. listened to races on the radio. Many weekends, that was as close as he was to his father. He liked listening to broadcasters talking about his dad. "A lot of my fondest memories were being a little kid and I had my Matchbox cars playing on the carpet while Dad was running the race," Earnhardt, Jr. said.[6]

It was also around that time that his father married for a third time. Earnhardt, Sr. and Teresa were married in 1982. By then, Earnhardt, Sr.'s winnings were more than $1 million. He and Teresa also owned a company. They called it Dale Earnhardt, Inc. It became extremely successful but was only two years old in 1982.

Earnhardt, Sr. had become more than a racing success. He had become a corporation. Earnhardt, Jr. and Kelley had become a family within a family.

"Dale Jr. and I stayed with nannies or relatives," Kelley told a newspaper reporter in 2006. "We didn't have that normal childhood, where the father comes home at 5 o'clock for dinner. It pretty much put Dale Jr. and me into survival mode."[7]

Their mother had moved to Norfolk, Virginia. She remarried and remained in Virginia for twenty years. Even though North Carolina shares a border with Virginia, it was a long drive to see Brenda. However, sometimes Brenda made the roundtrip in one day.

But most of the time, Earnhardt, Jr. was involved with his own childhood interests. Earnhardt, Jr. knew his father

DID YOU KNOW?

Dale Earnhardt, Sr. won seven NASCAR points championships.

loved him and his sister. He credits Earnhardt, Sr. for working so hard. Without that hard work, the Earnhardts would not have been so fortunate.

AWAKENING TO RACING

Earnhardt, Jr. took more notice of his father's career in coming years. Maybe he was making up for lost time. Maybe he started to sense his own future. Either way, he was taking notice. How could he not? His father was about to become the most famous racecar driver in the country. Earnhardt, Sr. was on the verge of dominating his sport.

Between his 1980 title run and 1984, Earnhardt, Sr. had not won more than two races in a season. He was, however, a top-ten driver. From 1984 until the end of his career, he finished at least that high sixteen times.

Earnhardt, Sr. settled into the No. 3 car in 1984. He also had a new permanent owner. That man was Richard Childress. They had worked together in previous seasons. The arrangement began a stretch of eight straight years in which Earnhardt, Sr. finished in the top ten.

That 1984 season provided a hint of things to come. In 1985, he won four races. He won five more in 1986 and a stunning eleven in 1987. He finished first in points in 1986 and 1987. Earnhardt, Jr. had entered his teenage years. By then, he had some experience with go-karts. He did not have his father's success, but he had fun. He ran them hard. He wiped out a lot. And he loved it.

Earnhardt, Sr. did not.

"I was about 12, and I was still kind of a little guy," Earnhardt, Jr. recalled in 2006. "I fell out of a go-kart so much, my daddy made me stop."[8]

However, Earnhardt, Jr.'s interest in racing could not be stopped. When he was thirteen, he told Earnhardt, Sr. how badly he wanted to race. He was not even close to earning his driver's license then. That did not matter to him. It did not even matter that he seemed to spend more time being thrown kart-wheeling from his go-kart than running it.

Earnhardt, Jr. was going to drive a racecar. It was just a matter of time.

"I just could not comprehend having to wait three more years. I was about to go crazy," he said. "I had never wanted something or craved anything as bad ever before. He just told me, 'Man, you've got to be patient.'"[9]

DID YOU KNOW? Dale Earnhardt, Sr. won four consecutive races in 1987.

RACING DAYS

Teenagers often struggle with patience. When a teen's dream is to fly through the gears, slam the shifter to high, mash the pedal, and scream toward an engine's limits, waiting may seem even more difficult.

This was the case for Earnhardt, Jr. He knew what he wanted, and he wanted it more than anything. He wanted to sit on the nose of a rocket and race it. The desire to become a professional racecar driver would come much later. At that point, however, the urge to drive was immediate.

He had the will. He lacked the means. He sure did not lack a role model.

Earnhardt, Sr. kept winning races and adding to what would become his legend. That also meant he was away from home a lot.

Earnhardt, Jr. missed him.

A GROWING LEGEND

In 1987, Earnhardt, Sr. won five of NASCAR's first seven races. *The New York Times* reported that he led more than half of the first 2,687 laps of the season. No other competitor came close to leading that many laps.

Back then, Earnhardt, Jr. might have been happy with just taking a lap.

However, the success of Earnhardt, Sr. powered Earnhardt, Jr. Like any adolescent, he was learning from his elders. Under his home's roof, Earnhardt, Jr. had one of the best resources in the world.

NASCAR did not make many racers millionaires back then. Earnhardt, Sr. was one of the first. He was a hardworking, self-made millionaire. He paid as many dues as anyone ever had. He gambled on his talents and won big.

On the track, it seemed Earnhardt, Sr. had a magic touch to go along with good old-fashioned brute force. Sometimes, he worked the magic. Other times, he and his car were blunter.

He did not shy away from being blunt. It came as naturally to him as driving.

Dale Earnhardt, Sr. smiles in Victory Lane in 1995.

Earnhardt, Sr. had a swagger. His steely stare could part traffic. He did not give an inch on the racetrack. He would rather take that inch and plow through to Victory Lane.

To fans, Earnhardt, Sr. was becoming an icon. By 1988, he had moved into the black car that he would drive the rest of his career. It led to the nickname, "The Man in Black." He had already been stuck with "The Intimidator." Both were appropriate on the track.

WAITING IMPATIENTLY

To Earnhardt, Jr., his father was an unrelenting and powerful influence. He was a hero. Earnhardt, Jr. might have followed him down any career path.

"I think that no matter what my father would've or could've been, whether it was a plumber or a carpenter, I would've followed in his footsteps," Junior said in 2002. "I really loved my father so much that I wanted to try to be just like him."[1]

Odds are both would have made excellent plumbers or carpenters—or just about anything else they wanted to be. But, as NASCAR's luck would have it, they were racecar drivers. But back then, only Earnhardt, Sr. was.

His son waited impatiently. Earnhardt, Jr. had racing in his heart. He had a champion's bloodlines. Growling motors were being built in an expanding race shop on his father's property. Cars gleamed in an immaculate garage area. Surrounding Earnhardt, Jr. were fast cars and a dream that seemed too far away.

Earnhardt, Jr. was like most of his young teenaged peers. Having a rich and famous father did not change that. Sometimes, it hurt. He was smallish and thin and occasionally awkward. He tried to fit in, but it did not always work.

He has often said he was either shy or a loner or that he was picked on. Life in those days was not easy for him.

His no-nonsense dad, on the other hand, was a little different than some fathers. He was a famous tough guy. He could be quite strict. And Earnhardt, Jr. had crossed him.

Soon, Earnhardt, Sr. took away some of his son's freedoms.

MILITARY SCHOOL

Earnhardt, Jr. had been acting up in school. His father answered with consequences. He sent Earnhardt, Jr. to Oak Ridge Military Academy, a school founded in 1852. As trying as life could be living with his father, Earnhardt, Jr.'s military school was also demanding.

It was also more than a two-hour drive from his father's house. Sometimes, Earnhardt, Jr. did not go home for the weekends. His support system, again, was Kelley. She enrolled at the school, too. Kelley had always felt like her brother's first line of defense.

The two remain close. Earnhardt, Jr. trusts few people as much as his sister. Their relationship is especially strong. It has been for many years.

Kelley always looked out for her younger brother.

"Dale Jr. was always littler than everybody—shy, got picked on a lot at school—and I was always the caretaker for anything he needed," Kelley said. "He borrowed lunch money from me. I did his chores when he wasn't in the mood to do them and would have gotten in trouble. I was always the mother hen."[2]

Earnhardt, Jr. found military school gave him a chance to mature. Oak Ridge also taught him some lessons. He is grateful when he looks back. He might not long for those days, but he remains appreciative.

In fact, as an adult in 2001, he wrote, "It was a crucial turning point in my life."[3]

Oak Ridge cadets woke up early. There were drills, formations, straight lines, and discipline. Shoes and brass had to be shined. Officers were saluted. Tradition and order were as established as the school's mission itself.

"I will always believe that I was 10 times the person after that experience," he said of his year-and-a-half at Oak Ridge.[4]

Afterward, Earnhardt, Jr. left to become a freshman at Mooresville High School in Mooresville, North Carolina. It was a more typical high school. Still, Mooresville came with its share of life lessons. Those continued to shape Earnhardt, Jr.

He was not one of the most popular kids. He had to find his own way.

Racing would provide a perfect distraction.

SWEET SIXTEEN

The alarm was about to ring. After years and years of the clock ticking down, Earnhardt, Jr.'s sixteenth birthday approached. He could climb into a car. He wasted little time.

How he finally arrived on the racing scene is now a part of history. At sixteen, Junior sold a go-kart. With the $500 he made, he bought a $200 car. It was a 1978 Monte Carlo.

He partnered with his half-brother, Kerry Earnhardt, to form a racing team. Five years older, Kerry had been reintroduced to the family a few years earlier. Together, the half-brothers would introduce themselves to racing.

They built that Monte Carlo into a car they could race. They even took turns driving it at tracks. Some siblings might have seen the situation as a competition but not Earnhardt, Jr. and Kerry. After all, the two of them had constructed a serious machine from a $200 junkyard car that was more than ten years old. They shared the labor of a new love.

DID YOU KNOW?

Dale Earnhardt, Jr. and his first racing partner, half-brother Kerry Earnhardt, made $300 by selling a go-kart and buying a car they would rebuild and race.

The car needed major upgrades. It was not race-ready. It needed a roll cage for structure. It needed a seat for racing. It needed a number painted on it. The work could be exhausting. In the process, Earnhardt, Jr. and Kerry learned how to build a car. They learned to fix a car. They learned a great deal, and they were doing it together.

Dale Earnhardt, Jr., left, Dale Earnhardt, Sr., center, and Kerry Earnhardt face reporters at a press conference.

Though the half-brothers were not raised in the same house, they were still family.

"We didn't grow up together, so we didn't have any animosities toward each other about anything in the past," Earnhardt, Jr. said. "We didn't know who was better and that never came into our minds.

"I didn't even think I was going to be a racecar driver."[5]

No one did. Back then, it was a hobby. Later, it grew into something more. Earnhardt, Sr.'s profession, plus Earnhardt, Jr.'s interest, equaled the seeds of something big. Yet none of it happened overnight.

PLANTING THE SEED

Around the same time as the boys were building their car, Earnhardt, Sr. made a suggestion. It was subtle but influential. Earnhardt, Jr. walked into his father's shop to find the sports section of the *Charlotte Observer* on a table. The paper advertised a race series opening in Concord, North Carolina, not far from Kannapolis and Mooresville.

"He said, 'If you want to race, here's a relatively cheap way to get into it, and if you like it, you'll find out this way,'" Earnhardt, Jr. recalled. "He was just laying an opportunity out there for me."[6]

The suggestion was simple and thoughtful. It was also clear and direct. Earnhardt, Sr. was likely trying to show his son he had options that many others did not. It was up to Earnhardt, Jr. to take advantage of them.

Earnhardt, Jr. wound up taking the opportunity. He raced his Monte Carlo as a street stock in Concord. He was finally competing. As much as he enjoyed the experience, however, racing as a career did not occur to him right away.

After graduating from Mooresville High, he went to Mitchell Community College. He studied for his automotive degree. Earnhardt, Sr. always wanted his kids to finish high school. Earnhardt, Jr. did not let him down. He learned even more about cars at Mitchell. He earned his college degree on top of his high school diploma.

Since he was not racing for a living, he took a job at his father's car dealership in Newton, North Carolina. Junior worked as a mechanic. He changed oil—fast. He brags, jokingly, that he became one of the quickest oil-changers at the business.

"I ended up getting a job at the dealership," he said. "I went all over the dealership to learn about [the operation] because I figured that was probably where I was going to end up."[7]

Of course, Earnhardt, Jr. ended up a long way from there. It took a little while. While working at the shop, his racing was limited.

Earnhardt, Jr. enjoyed working on cars. He had fun with his friends at work. And he enjoyed the regular existence. He might not have taken to the regular hours, but he was still young.

In those days, he made a fraction of what he could make in a last-place finish on a Sunday on the racetrack. Though his salary was not much, he was not complaining much, either.

4

SHOWING PROMISE

Street stocks indulged Earnhardt, Jr.'s love of racing. However, racing on that circuit for a couple of seasons, he could not earn a living. In his later teens, however, his love would become his living.

Until that point, Earnhardt, Sr. was a guiding force. He was not actively pushing Earnhardt, Jr. toward NASCAR stardom. The two merely shared a common interest. It would develop into something much deeper, but it had a ways to go.

Earnhardt, Jr. was still young. He was either in school or working at the dealership in those days.

Earnhardt, Sr. was often on the road, racing. Even when he was home, he was not always available to his son. Earnhardt, Sr. might be out working on his car. Or he might have been concentrating on some of the many things on his own plate.

At other times, Earnhardt, Jr. might be working on his own car. Rather than teaching him how to fix it, Earnhardt, Sr. let his son figure a lot out on his own.

Earnhardt, Sr. was a dad. He was also a hero to Earnhardt, Jr. Still, Junior's racing career needed a little more guidance. He needed a mentor.

Enter Gary Hargett.

A GUIDING HAND

Hargett is yet another old-school tough guy in Earnhardt, Jr.'s life. Before tutoring race drivers, Hargett was a pig farmer. Earnhardt, Sr. trusted him with his son, and with good reason.

Hargett had known Ralph Earnhardt since the 1960s. He teamed with Earnhardt, Sr.—in a No. 8 car—during his early days. And he would help Earnhardt, Jr. in his quest to make a career of racing.

Earnhardt, Jr. looked back on Hargett's influence in 2004. "I used to work with a guy named Gary Hargett . . . and he got to be like a grandfather to me," Junior said. "I couldn't imagine going to the racetrack without him."[1]

Racecars in the late model divisions look like NASCAR cars. Dale Earnhardt, Jr., began racing late model cars in 1992.

By then, Earnhardt, Jr. was no stranger to the tracks in the South. He had raced his street stock and was finding his way. He had also attended a stock car-racing school run by Andy Hillenburg.

In addition to a mentor, Earnhardt, Jr. could also use some finesse. His early goals on the track seemed limited to one thing: Go fast. That was how he drove go-karts, too. It did not always work with stock cars. Finishing first is the key, but getting there takes skill as well as speed.

Hargett had made Earnhardt, Sr. aware that he would let Junior drive a car on what was called the late model circuit. That was a step up for sure. At first, it was just a few races in 1992, the year Earnhardt, Jr.

turned eighteen years old. After that, until 1996, Junior made a run through whole late model seasons.

EARNING HIS PLACE

The late model division is not what the name might suggest. The cars were not from old black and white movies. They did not have shiny, spoked rims or low-lying roofs and skinny

DID YOU KNOW?

Prior to mentoring Dale Earnhardt, Jr., Gary Hargett had worked not only with Dale Earnhardt, Sr. but also with Ralph Earnhardt.

white-walled tires. The drivers did not wear leather helmets and whip scarves around their necks at the starting line.

The cars were just a couple of years old. They had loud engines, sleek bodies, metal armor, thick roll cages, and wide tires. They looked like modern racecars. In fact, at the time, they might have looked more like racecars than Earnhardt, Jr. looked like a racecar driver. In one early picture, Earnhardt, Jr. leans next to his green No. 3 car. He looks as light as a breeze. He barely filled out his racing suit. His hat looks too big. Under it, his reddish-blonde hair was cut short on the top and long in the back. It was the way teens wore their hair in the early 1990s.

Earnhardt, Jr.'s late model cars, such as the hulking No. 8 he made famous in the top division, were supported by Earnhardt, Sr. In 1994, Earnhardt, Jr.'s father began a company called Chance Racing. Earnhardt, Jr., Kelley, and Kerry all raced in the late model division with help from Chance.

One thing Earnhardt, Sr. did not do was hold his kids' hands out at the track. All three were just beginning. They worked for outside sponsorship.

Those days provided another great learning experience for Earnhardt, Jr. He worked on his own car. He had done that with the street stock but not like this. He learned how to prepare a car for a race.

With stock cars, adjustments have to be made to suit conditions. Some tracks require different setups than others. In the big leagues of racing, those adjustments are made by a crew. The driver has input, and the team makes the changes. In the lower divisions, the driver turns many of his own wrenches.

"During this stretch of my career, I was a one-man team. I always drove my own equipment and did much of the work myself," he said.[2]

LIVING WITH A FAMOUS NAME

There were lots of differences then. Earnhardt, Jr. was not a superstar. Even worse, his father was.

In ten years, Junior would be among the most popular drivers in NASCAR. In the early 1990s, however, he was one of the least liked on the track. He was Dale Earnhardt, Jr., son of a legend. Even though he was not racing in Concord anymore, that name made sure he could not hide.

As soon as he threaded that thin frame through the driver's window, he wore a target. The No. 3 on the side might well have been a bull's-eye.

Earnhardt, Jr. opened his career with Hargett racing in Myrtle Beach, South Carolina. The track was a four-hour drive from where the Earnhardts lived. Being away from the Earnhardts' backyard seemed like a good idea.

Unfortunately, the name Earnhardt is not like the name Jones. It tends to stand out, especially in racing country.

The late model circuit could be unforgiving. Being Dale Earnhardt, Jr., or even Dale Earnhardt, Sr., did not guarantee anything. It helped, but there were no sure things. Being Earnhardt, Jr. came with an added stigma. Some thought he was spoiled. They were often wrong, but that did not matter.

Drivers are competitive by nature. They want to win. They want to be the best on the track. And they want to beat the best.

If they could not beat the best, beating his son would do. Making Earnhardt, Jr.'s life difficult in the process became a pastime for some during Junior's late model career. Racers did not mind treating Dale Earnhardt's youngest son poorly on the track. There were cheap shots. There was taunting. Earnhardt, Jr.

was small, and he looked young. Hargett helped him through those times. He did not treat Earnhardt, Jr. delicately. Military school helped Earnhardt, Jr. grow as a person. Hargett helped Earnhardt, Jr. grow as a person and a driver.

"When I started driving for him, I was young and self-centered," Earnhardt, Jr. said. "But he and his volunteer crew gave me no breaks because of who I was."[3]

Hargett and Earnhardt, Jr. were together through 1995.

GROWING UP

Overall, the wins did not come as quickly as Earnhardt, Jr. wanted. He wound up making 113 late model starts. He won only three races. The first late model win came on August 20, 1994, at Myrtle Beach Speedway.

He almost always made a good showing. He finished in the top ten 90 times. He finished in the top five almost 60 times. The races were mostly held on short tracks. Neither the crowds nor the payoffs were big.

But Earnhardt, Jr. proved himself there. He was maturing—and so was his driving. That was enough to catch the eyes of the racing world.

Earnhardt, Jr. was gaining a reputation, too. He was thought of as a good racecar driver who mostly kept to himself.

TRACK FACT
Dale Earnhardt, Jr.'s first start in the top minor league was at the Carolina Pride 250.

He was growing into adulthood. He was becoming his own man. Soon, he would be ready for another big challenge.

The highest rung of the NASCAR minor leagues waited.

In 1995, Earnhardt, Jr. moved away from Hargett, leaving another comfort zone behind. He moved closer to home. There, he could concentrate on becoming a bigger part of his father's racing operation. That operation, Dale Earnhardt, Inc., is also known as DEI.

"I definitely had to work my way up the ranks," Earnhardt, Jr. says. "I would hope that people would look at my accomplishments and realize that I have had to make a name for myself."[4]

It was like he was learning the family business—but not exactly with the family. Earnhardt, Jr. was learning on the road. He was getting his fingers dirty. He was finding out how to approach different tracks. It takes diverse skills to drive a long track and a short track. Driving requires varied skills for sharp corners

When Earnhardt, Jr. first raced the Busch series, he drove car number 31.

and long bends. Being in the driver's seat was the best classroom in the world for him.

Earnhardt, Jr. continued to race late models in 1996. He raced out of his father's shop. It was the most successful season he would have there.

That same year, he got his big break. He could debut in the highest-ranking minor league series. Even better, it was at Myrtle Beach. He knew the track well.

Earnhardt, Jr. qualified as the seventh fastest driver. The car was owned by his father. His race number was 31. In the race, he finished fourteenth.

Earnhardt, Sr. watched on television the day before his race at Michigan International Speedway.

That was on June 22, 1996. Earnhardt, Jr. only finished with $1,880 in winnings, but he jumped a hurdle.

The path to racing at the highest level had been cleared for yet another step.

Earnhardt, Jr.'s racing days were no longer part of a hobby. It did not matter that he was not even twenty-three years old. Unlike his father, he was single at that age. It would be easier to chase the racing dream that way.

His older sister had gone off to college. His older brother focused on his own growing family.

All three were living in grown-up worlds. Earnhardt, Jr. was no longer the fair-haired and wispy teen. It was not the early 1990s anymore, and his hat did not look too big on his head.

He had talent. He had financial backing. He had potential. And he had grown up a bit.

By the late 1990s, he was, in short, a racecar driver.

Life was changing for Earnhardt, Jr. It would not ever look the same again. Once he hit NASCAR's top minor league, he was an instant curiosity. Soon after, he would become a star there.

Earnhardt, Jr. entered the 1997 season at the age of twenty-two. He prepared for a limited schedule in that top minor league. That meant he would race only eight times.

Mostly, the series runs on Saturdays. Often, those races are held at the same track as the top series. Instead of running little short tracks in front of dozens of fans, the racers perform in front of tens of thousands. Some tracks hold more than one hundred thousand people.

DID YOU KNOW?

Even a car in NASCAR's top minor league generates well above 600 horsepower.

Racers from the top NASCAR circuit sometimes race there, too. It is yet another incentive for fans to attend Saturday races. They get to watch the stars of the future and the present at the same time.

The cars driven on Saturday are more manageable. At least, they are designed to be. They are shorter and wider, and they do not have as much power.

The Saturday races are not as long as races on the top circuit. For example, instead of running 500 miles on a Sunday at a speedway in Concord, North Carolina, drivers will run 300 miles at the same track on Saturday.

Earnhardt, Jr. raced eight times in 1997. Usually he drove a No. 31 car. DEI owned his car. He had an outside sponsor, but his owner, again, was his father, Dale Earnhardt, Sr.

MAKING A LIVING AS A DRIVER

Unfortunately, Earnhardt, Jr.'s first few races did not turn out well. He finished thirty-ninth in his first two starts. In his third start, he was thirty-eighth. In that third race, his winnings were $11,400.

Even then, it was clear Earnhardt, Jr. could make a living. During the course of the 1997 season, he made more than $50,000. That was in limited action.

One prominent moment came on August 22, 1997. He qualified second in Bristol, Tennessee. He finished twenty-second in that race. His highest finish that season was seventh.

During 1997, Earnhardt, Jr. was often racing inferior equipment. As he recalled in *Driver #8*, he was getting by with "a couple of low-budget teams and an old car that DEI had lying around."[1]

The top equipment went to DEI's top driver on that circuit. By then, the DEI operation was big. It consisted of race teams, a giant shop, and many cars. But Earnhardt, Jr. did not get first pick just because he was Earnhardt, Jr.

According to Tony Eury, Earnhardt, Jr. had to overcome mechanical disadvantages. Eury was a crew member for the top member of the DEI stable.

"Dale Jr. always had the second-best car, always had an engine that wasn't as good as ours, always worked on it himself, just him and a couple of young guys from his late-model team," Eury said.[2]

At the end of the 1997 season, Earnhardt, Jr. ranked forty-seventh in points. In his last three races of 1997, he finished thirty-fourth, sixteenth, and thirteenth. He was improving.

Earnhardt, Jr. had shown promise at every level. Now twenty-three years old, he seemed ripe for a full-time ride in the top minor league circuit.

His father thought so, too.

AN EXCITING PROMOTION

Luckily, there was an opening for a driver at DEI.

It all happened because of the previous driver's success. In 1997, Steve Park was a good driver for DEI. In a white-and-blue No. 3 car, he finished twenty-one of thirty races in the top ten. Over the last eight races of the season, his average finish was 3.5.

Park was due for a promotion. He got one, and he made history.

The first driver to race a full-time DEI-owned car on NASCAR's top circuit was Park. Earnhardt, Sr. still drove a car owned by Childress. This meant Earnhardt, Sr. would race against a car his company owned.

It also meant a few other things. It meant that DEI was growing again. It also resulted in an opening inside the white-and-blue No. 3 car. Earnhardt, Sr. asked Earnhardt, Jr. if he wanted that seat.

"I couldn't believe it!" Earnhardt, Jr. said.[3] He was going to drive a No. 3 car in 1998. He was only one step from NASCAR's big leagues.

His first response was excitement. He remembered all those times he had walked around his family's big, beautiful shop, all those times he had seen a fleet of gleaming racecars he could not drive, all those times he had longed for his father's blessing as a driver.

After all those years of staring a racing career in the face, of working his way up in the ranks, and turning his own wrenches and paying his dues, Earnhardt, Jr. finally had his own high-profile car and team.

Not only was it a team, it was also family. Tony Eury and Earnhardt, Sr. had married sisters. That made Eury an uncle to Earnhardt, Jr.

DID YOU KNOW?

Dale Earnhardt, Jr. did not sign an official contract with his father until 1998.

Tony also had a son. His name is Tony Eury, Jr. Earnhardt, Jr. and Eury, Jr. are cousins. On the No. 3 team, Eury, Sr. was the crew chief. Eury, Jr. was also involved with the race team on a daily basis.

It set the wheels in motion for one incredible ride. Not that Earnhardt, Sr. ever let Earnhardt, Jr. feel really comfortable with the decision. Earnhardt, Sr., again, probably did not want to just hand something to his son.

Dale Earnhardt, Jr. talks with Tony Eury, Jr. during practice.

"I didn't know for sure that I was the driver until the name decals came into the shop two weeks before Daytona," Earnhardt, Jr. said.[4]

He was excited, but he was also nervous. The drivers of the car he was about to take over won races. Before Steve Park, Jeff Green was successful, too.

Earnhardt, Jr. was concerned he would not live up to expectations. After all, it was going to be the best car he had ever driven. He would get the best engines and the best cars. He was also with the best crew he had ever had.

He could have failed.

He didn't—not by a long shot.

A ROCKY START

Earnhardt, Jr. was flat-out awesome. Well, maybe he was not exactly great right out of the gate.

His first race in 1998 was at Daytona International Speedway. It was the Saturday race before the "Great American Race." His father had once won the Saturday opener five straight years.

Earnhardt, Jr.'s luck was not that good on February 14. He qualified third, but the race would not end well. He finished only 81 of the 120 laps. He also bowed out with a spectacular crash that sent him flipping in the air. He recalled the experience as seeing, "Earth, sky, earth, sky, earth, sky."[5]

After that, he did not feel well, and he returned home. Yet another bittersweet day would follow.

On February 15, 1998, Earnhardt, Sr. won the Great American Race. It was his twentieth start, but he had never won that race before. He was one of the most decorated drivers ever. He had won more races at the track than anyone, but he had not won the biggest race there—until now.

But Earnhardt, Jr. had missed his father's

DID YOU KNOW?

Dale Earnhardt, Sr. won a record thirty-four races at Daytona International Speedway, but he failed to win the Daytona 500 until 1998.

Dale Earnhardt, Sr. jumps out of his car in Victory Lane at the Daytona 500 in 1998.

biggest moment. Heading home to Mooresville remains one of Earnhardt, Jr.'s favorite activities. He might have traded all the good times there for sticking around in Daytona one more day.

Earnhardt, Sr. winning the Daytona 500 was one of the biggest stories in sports. The Intimidator was nearing fifty years old, and he pulled off the win.

When he won, crew chiefs from other teams came out to congratulate him. He had lost that race so many times and so many ways. In his twentieth run, he was a sentimental favorite.

"It worked out to be the right place and the right time," Earnhardt, Sr. said. "It was my time. I've been passed here. I've run out of gas. I've been cut with a tire. I've done it all. I wrote the book, and this is the last chapter. We finally won the Daytona 500."[6]

Earnhardt, Sr. also had some inspiration beyond the obvious. It came the day before. It was the day his son finished poorly in the Saturday race. It was also a day when he received a token from a Make-A-Wish Foundation child. A little girl had given him a penny.

"She gave me this penny," Earnhardt, Sr. said. "She said, 'I rubbed this penny, and this is going to win you the Daytona 500.' I glued that penny to my dashboard and it's still on my dashboard."[7]

FINDING SUCCESS

Earnhardt, Sr.'s win kicked off a life-changing year for Earnhardt, Jr., too. In only his third full-time race, Junior finished second. That race was held in Las Vegas. There, he won $59,000. It was the biggest payday of his career. That was on February 28, 1998.

Two weeks later, the circuit moved to Nashville. Earnhardt, Jr. finished third. A tenth and a second followed. Earnhardt, Jr. was picking up momentum.

Earnhardt, Sr. wins the 1998 Daytona 500.

On April 4, 1998, the twenty-three-year-old hit another milestone. He won his first race on the circuit. It was at Texas Motor Speedway. He won in only his sixteenth career NASCAR start. That was the same number of races it took his father to win.

In Victory Lane, Earnhardt, Jr. thrust his right arm into the air and roared to punctuate the win.

Earnhardt, Sr. was there to see it, too. He would drive the following day at the same track. The two embraced after the race.

The New York Times joked that Earnhardt, Sr. cried again for only the second time in 1998. The first was when he won at Daytona. The second was when his son scored his first NASCAR victory there in Texas.

For his part, Earnhardt, Jr. was also moved. It was an emotional day.

"It stirred memories of the years I had tried so hard to earn my dad's approval," he said not long after the win. "Maybe that did it. It really was a proud moment for him, to show that much excitement and happiness over something that I had accomplished."[8]

GOING TO THE TOP

Earnhardt, Jr. was just getting started. As always, however, he would take a few steps backward before going forward. His next few weeks were not his best.

Then, afterward, he took off.

From about the midpoint of that season on, he was the top driver on the track. Twelve top-five finishes followed. That run included an incredible six more wins. His winnings totaled more than $830,000. He also had the chance to race against his older brother on three occasions.

In June 1998, he signed an official contract with his father. Until then, the two were going on an informal contract. Earnhardt, Jr. was making only $500 a week and a cut of his winnings. In September, Earnhardt, Jr. signed another contract. This one was an even bigger deal. It was a contract to drive in the "Show."

He would be driving in the top NASCAR series, the same one his dad was in. The series that raced on Sundays. The one that TV networks covered. It was one of the hottest properties in sports.

Earnhardt, Jr. would only run a handful of races in 1999, but he had a sponsor locked up then and into the future. The contract ran through the 2004 season.

It was quite a year for Earnhardt, Jr. He capped off 1998 with the Busch series crown. In the process, he became the first third-generation champion of a NASCAR division.

Ralph Earnhardt went first. Earnhardt, Sr. followed. Earnhardt, Jr. continued the tradition.

Now Earnhardt, Jr. was a champion in his own right.

With one national minor-league NASCAR series championship in his back pocket, Earnhardt, Jr. found yet another gear. He dominated the series again. He also jumped in to wet his feet in the top stock car circuit in the land. It is now known as the Nextel Cup series.

In 1999, Junior was still young, but he was more at ease. He was more comfortable with himself, with his father, and with his place in the world. He certainly was not complacent. The will to win was still burning.

The season started slowly. Earnhardt, Jr. scored only one top-ten finish in the first four races. Then the season picked up speed. As in 1998, he finished near the top of races. In 1999, he was even more consistent.

Winning races wins headlines. Finishing consistently wins titles. Earnhardt, Jr. found that in 1998. He improved on it in 1999.

With an average finish of 9.9, he earned more than $985,000. In time, he would jump to the points lead and never look back.

TRACK FACT

In 1998, Dale Earnhardt, Jr. finished among the top three in fourteen races.

MEDIA FRENZY

The 1999 season was notable for a couple of reasons. For one, Earnhardt, Jr. locked down his second straight title in the Busch series. He had to overcome that tough start, too. He did all of this knowing he would make his debut in the top circuit.

Earnhardt, Jr. was going to run in his first "Cup" race. Not only would he race in one, he would race in five. But the first one was a biggie.

The question on so many minds was going to be answered. Could the kid drive a Cup car? As Jeff MacGregor said in *Sports Illustrated*, "Sure, he'd won two championships in [NASCAR's minor leagues], but did he have the grit, the steel, the mud, to run in the Show?"[1]

On May 30, Earnhardt, Jr. made one of the most anticipated starts in the history of NASCAR. And he did it at Charlotte, the track nearest his home. It was also where his dad had debuted.

A new-generation star, Earnhardt, Jr. understood the hype machine. He did not have to like it, but he understood it.

He may have put the situation best himself in *Driver #8*:

"Imagine being the son of Michael Jordan and then becoming a number one draft pick (chosen by a team owned by your father) after winning two consecutive NCAA titles."[2]

That first game would come with some nerves. Earnhardt, Jr. and his father even appeared on the cover of a 2000 commemorative issue of *Sports Illustrated*. The heading read, "FIERY FAMILY."

Prior to the race, Earnhardt, Jr.'s qualifying time was better than Earnhardt, Sr.'s. That became a big story heading into the weekend. Earnhardt, Jr.'s new car number matched his position. The No. 8 had qualified an impressive eighth.

On May 29, Earnhardt, Jr. ran the Saturday race at Lowe's Motor Speedway in Concord, North Carolina. He finished second.

TRACK FACT
In 1999, Dale Earnhardt, Jr. finished
among the top three in sixteen races.

The next day and the next step drew near. So did his anxiety.

"We've been planning and thinking about this for months," Earnhardt, Jr. said that day, "and it feels good to actually get out on the track and do something. I think everyone has that fear [of failure] in the back of their mind when they're getting ready to do something really important."[3]

Earnhardt, Jr. climbed into the seat for his first Cup race at the track.

For Earnhardt, Jr., the No. 8 was painted on the side in white. His car was bright red. Around 200,000 people were in attendance. If everyone was looking at him, he was not hard to find.

His belts were latched. His helmet was fastened, and his goggles were set. The steering wheel was popped into place. Butterflies were as much a part of his gear as the roll cage and engine. They protected him and drove him in some ways.

It would be the longest race of his life. This particular Cup race covers 600 miles. On Saturdays, Earnhardt, Jr.

Dale Earnhardt, Jr.'s average starting position in the top circuit during 1999 was 14.4.

rarely had to run more than 300 miles.

His first Cup start taught him many lessons. His car was not perfect. He was understandably nervous. He was getting used to the new surroundings.

He had more than 40 of the best drivers on the track. One of them was his car's owner and his dad. There was a lot of pressure. Much of it, Earnhardt, Jr. put on himself.

On one stop, he had trouble finding his own pit area. In the end, he finished sixteenth.

During the course of his five Cup races, he would finish better—tenth at Richmond and fourteenth at Atlanta—and worse—twenty-fourth at Michigan and forty-third at New Hampshire.

In any event, he was ready to leave the minor leagues behind. Earnhardt, Jr. was the most popular driver in the minors. No one had more media attention or autograph-seekers.

In 1999, *Stock Car Racing Magazine* captured the phenomenon.

"This is just rolling along and snowballing and we're going to see how far down the hill," Earnhardt, Jr. said. "I don't know whether to slow it down, to stop it for a minute, to take a break, to keep going, to

After joining the NASCAR circuit in 1999, Earnhardt, Jr. quickly became one of NASCAR's most popular drivers.

speed it up. I don't really know because I don't have any experience with this."[4]

Where Earnhardt, Jr. did have experience was on the track. He was the most popular driver, and the circuit's most successful in 1998 and 1999.

The time came to leave yet another stepping stone behind. Whether Earnhardt, Jr. was ready or not, the biggest stock car racing stage was holding a place for him.

HIS OWN MAN

But his father was not about to gush. To the media, Earnhardt, Sr. talked about how his son would be just another racer to beat.

WHAT A RUN: 1999

Race week	Start	Finish
13	3	2
14	22	2
15	15	1
16	1	1
17	3	1

"He always has some way of putting you down," Earnhardt, Jr. told *Stock Car Racing Magazine* in 1999. "That makes me keep crawling to get to the top. . . . He goes out of his way to make things more difficult because he believes, in the long run, I'll be a better person for it."[5]

Earnhardt, Sr. was not as light and carefree as some fathers. His way was appreciated by Earnhardt, Jr. as time wore on.

The father-son dynamic added to the hype. Many parents teach their children valuable lessons. Sometimes the lessons are difficult. Sometimes they may even be harsh. Children might want to rebel. It is not often the process plays itself out in front of cameras in a professional sport.

And just because his name was Dale Earnhardt, Jr. did not mean his life was easy.

"Being the son of a famous driver like my dad definitely gets attention and helps open some doors," Junior said. "On the other hand, I have to deal with things that other drivers my age don't have to deal with. Because I'm named Dale Earnhardt, a lot of fans expect me to be able to drive like my father, and that's not realistic. Sometimes I feel pressured to live up to their expectations. I put a lot of pressure on myself."[6]

He has always put pressure on himself. In 2000, Earnhardt, Jr. took that pressure with him to the Show. Uncle Tony and cousin Tony would take the ride with him.

Heading into 2000, it was clear Earnhardt, Jr. was developing his own spirit. He was different from his father, even if there were similarities.

As an indication of how popular he was, Earnhardt, Jr. was able to write a book about his rookie season. That book is called *Driver #8*.

In his intro, Junior says the season was full of emotions: "exhilaration and exhaustion, fun and fear, triumph and tragedy, and everything in between."[7]

The season opened, typically, in Daytona. The date was February 20. It marked Earnhardt, Jr.'s first Daytona 500. He had not even attended the race as a fan at that point.

That Daytona 500 provided another learning experience. He entered it with some self-doubt. The media fed into it. Was he ready for the big leagues?

DID YOU KNOW?

Dale Earnhardt, Jr. won three straight Busch series races in 1999—at Dover, South Boston, and Watkins Glen.

Could he race with the best? Could he beat the best? Would he win the Rookie of the Year award?

It was a lot to take on—and so were the crowds. Junior was mobbed almost everywhere he went.

However, he found his bravado. He had worked a lifetime for the moment, and he would enjoy it. He publicly embraced the idea that he was ready—that he had arrived. As he had done thousands of times before, he strapped himself into his racecar.

Earnhardt, Jr. prepares to get in his car for the start of the 2004 Mountain Dew Southern 500.

But this was much different for so many reasons. During the race, Earnhardt, Jr. and Earnhardt, Sr. ran together for a time. Circumstances led to Earnhardt, Jr. finishing thirteenth. Earnhardt, Sr. finished twenty-first. Other racers teamed up to leave them shuffled behind in the pack.

Earnhardt, Jr.'s interest in passing cars overshadowed his interest in working with other drivers to finish high in the standings. Old habits die hard.

But there was good news, besides the $107,775 payday. Earnhardt, Jr. was a Cup driver now. Yet that came with some bad news. He would have to keep proving himself every week.

A BIG WIN

Junior ran thirty-four races in 2000. The high point came at Texas Motor Speedway on April 2.

After Daytona, things had gone from bad to worse. In six weeks of racing, Junior's average finish to that point was around twenty-fourth. Times were rough. Heading into Texas, his previous three finishes were twenty-ninth, fortieth, and thirty-eighth.

As usual, Earnhardt, Jr. was rushed by autograph-seekers anyway.

He liked the Texas track. It was where he won his first NASCAR race back in 1998. On top of that, his No. 8 car that day was very good.

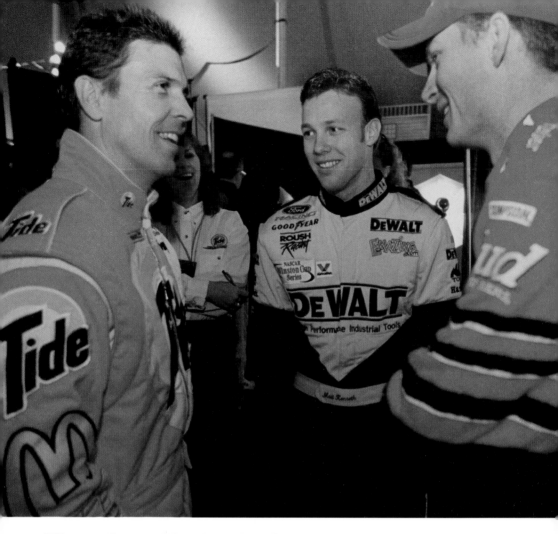

Winston Cup rookies, from left, Scott Pruett, Matt Kenseth, and Dale Earnhardt, Jr. chat during a photo session in 2000.

As it turned out, his car was the very best that day. Earnhardt, Jr. fell behind a few times. He also cruised to the lead a number of times. He and his crew avoided late-race mistakes, and the No. 8 DEI car had its first win. It was Earnhardt, Sr.'s first Cup win as an owner, and Earnhardt, Jr.'s first as a driver. Afterward, the two embraced.

"I just was glad to be there with him," Earnhardt, Sr. said. "It's just amazing. I'll see how big his head gets now."[8]

Maybe that last part was just to get the media going. Earnhardt, Jr. described a more emotional Earnhardt, Sr. after the race.

"I love you," Earnhardt, Sr. told his son. "I want to make sure you take this time to enjoy this and enjoy what you accomplished today. You can get so swept up with what's going on around you that you really don't enjoy yourself, so I want you to celebrate."[9]

And celebrate he did. Red, white, and blue confetti fell around him, and he thrust his right arm into the sky and hollered.

In post-race interviews, Earnhardt, Jr. immediately thanked his crew. He knew it was a team effort. He said his car did what he wanted it to do— and it was thanks to his uncle and cousin.

When journalists wanted to see Earnhardt, Jr. for more interviews, he made sure to take Eury, Jr. with him.

During one interview, Earnhardt, Jr. decided to admit some of his frailty.

"You can beat yourself up only so much before you take a lot of confidence away from yourself," he said.[10]

He was talking about that race, but he could have meant it at many points in his life.

Still, no one could take that win away. Earnhardt, Jr. had won a Cup race. It did not take long, however, before he and his team went back to work.

UPS AND DOWNS

There were other highs that season—and many lows. Among the highs was a month-long stretch beginning May 6. Earnhardt, Jr. won his second career Cup race on that day. The track was in Richmond. Earnhardt, Sr. and Earnhardt, Jr. were racing one-two for a bit before Earnhardt, Jr.'s pit strategy paid off for a win.

In a classic father-son moment, Earnhardt, Sr. told his son he loved him and congratulated him. Then he told his son to find his own way home.

"Big E waits for no one," Earnhardt, Jr. said.[11]

Before heading home, Earnhardt, Jr. again publicly thanked his crew.

He also saw his mother. Brenda watched Earnhardt, Jr.'s races in Richmond. Even if they had not seen each other for a long time, there were the races at Richmond. Brenda moved back to the Charlotte area not long afterward.

Then the circuit moved to an all-star event in Charlotte. Earnhardt, Jr. drove to a win. In this race, rookies were rarely entered, let alone winners. The race did not count toward point standings, but it sure counted to Earnhardt, Jr.—and not just because the winner's check was worth about $500,000.

Earnhardt, Jr.'s pit crew works on his car during a pit stop.

Earnhardt, Jr. dedicated the win to Adam Petty. Petty had died during a practice run a week earlier in New Hampshire. The loss had hit Earnhardt Jr. hard.

On May 28, the 600-mile event returned to Charlotte. Earnhardt, Jr. and his team qualified No. 1. It was their first pole position. Earnhardt, Sr. finished third in the race, with his son right behind him in fourth. Later that year, Earnhardt, Jr., Kerry, and Earnhardt, Sr. ran a race together in Michigan. Earnhardt, Jr. again qualified first, earning the pole position.

However, there were also a number of lows. Earnhardt, Jr. found out how grueling the Cup series could be. In all, Earnhardt, Jr. finished with five official top tens in 2000. It would not be enough to win the circuit's Rookie of the Year award. He finished sixteenth in the points standings. Old friend and fellow rookie Matt Kenseth finished fourteenth.

It was Kenseth who won the 600-mile race in May. Earnhardt, Jr. made sure to congratulate him.

Earnhardt, Jr. may not have won the rookie award, but he thrilled NASCAR fans into believing he was the future.

At one point, Earnhardt, Jr. raced for this opportunity. Now, he would be racing to keep it.

BITTERSWEET VICTORY

Earnhardt, Jr.'s 2000 season ended with a sixteenth-place finish, a couple of record-setting poles, a whole lot of press (including features in *Rolling Stone, People* magazine, and *Sports Illustrated*, plus the taping of an MTV special), and, like always, tons of promise.

In October 2000, he also wrote a column for nascar.com. It turned into a tribute to his father. It also spawned one of the more special moments in their lives.

The column was written from Earnhardt, Jr.'s point of view. It was from a son who saw a legend's life

Dale Earnhardt, Sr. hugs his son in Victory Lane on February 18, 2000. Dale Sr. won the International Race of Champions round at Daytona International Speedway.

unfold before him. "I've seen this man create many things. With no blueprints, he has carved and produced wonders upon wonders," Junior wrote.[1]

In the article, he says he wonders how his father has known so many things. Before Earnhardt fired the article off to nascar.com editors, he showed it to his father.

"He got up and walked right over to me, right in my face," Earnhardt, Jr. said. "He gave me a big hug and told me how much he liked it, and I thought for a second we were both gonna cry, which doesn't happen at all with the Earnhardt men."[2]

Earnhardt, Sr. told him it was so good it belonged in a book. It seemed that the two were achieving an adult relationship.

If only it could have continued.

LOSING HIS FATHER

The 2000 race season ended with a whimper for Earnhardt, Jr.

Before it was done, he was looking forward to his sophomore season.

"I can't wait to see what's ahead for 2001," he said.[3]

Sadly, the incident at the 2001 Daytona 500 broke the hearts of racing fans everywhere. Of course, the Earnhardt family was hardest hit—Earnhardt, Jr., in particular.

After a lifetime of finding his way into it, Earnhardt, Jr. had forged a fulfilling adult relationship with his father. Earnhardt, Sr. found a place where he talked about how proud he was of his son.

Then he was gone.

The news of Earnhardt, Sr.'s death was bigger than NASCAR. Almost every newspaper in the country made mention of the racing tragedy. President George W. Bush called Teresa Earnhardt to offer his condolences.

The grieving process would take a long time. At first, the Earnhardts grieved in private. Earnhardt, Jr. did not do much talking then. But he did race. In fact, he would climb into his cockpit sanctuary only seven days later. The race was at Rockingham, North Carolina.

Earnhardt, Jr. quietly listens to a fellow driver talk about his father at a news conference at North Carolina Speedway.

"We'll get through this," he said. "I'm sure he'd want us to keep going, and that's what we're going to do."[4]

When Earnhardt, Jr. held a press conference on February 23, it was just five days after the accident. He was quick to take blame off Sterling Marlin's shoulders. Marlin was the driver who collided with Earnhardt, Sr., which sent the black No. 3 into the wall.

At the next race, Earnhardt, Jr. crashed on the first lap. He finished forty-third. In some ways, Earnhardt, Jr. saw his new situation as a new beginning.

"I know it's only been a little more than a month," he said, "but I do a lot of things that I never did before, and I only do 'em because I know he wanted me to do 'em."[5]

Earnhardt, Jr. seemed to become more accountable. He seemed to become even more grown up. Earnhardt, Jr. has always seemed self-aware. He naturally seems to understand there is a difference between his truth and what people think. At times, it might be a distraction. He might care too often about what people think.

In many cases, that understanding pays off. He spends energy thinking about his place. After the crash, Waltrip asked him whether he felt a lot of pressure to live up to his father's accomplishments.

"People have always asked me that," Earnhardt, Jr. said, "and maybe it's more relevant now than it was before, but I don't feel a lot of pressure to equal any of his success or anything like that. Or try to be personally what he was or be a reminder to people. I mean, that is an awful lot to ask of somebody, and it's really unhealthy."[6]

At almost every turn, Earnhardt, Jr. finds a way to come off as his own man. One thing made those turns even more difficult. At the time, racetracks and fans wanted to honor his father. Everywhere he went, Earnhardt, Jr. was reminded of losing Earnhardt, Sr.

At one track, a No. 3 had been painted in the grass. It was 50 feet (15 meters) high and impossible to miss.

One place where Earnhardt, Jr. could escape was his car.

"It must be hard to come in here, and see all the memorials and listen to what all the people are saying and not be affected by it," said Ty Norris of DEI. "Maybe that is the best time of his day, when he's in that racecar."[7]

EMOTIONAL WINS

That season, Earnhardt, Jr. won three races. It was a remarkable total under the circumstances of 2001. He won at Daytona in July, at Dover in September, and Talladega in October.

Fans pass a large number three on the side of the track where Earnhardt, Sr. was killed.

The first win of the three was by far the most emotional—and with good reason.

During the long NASCAR season, some tracks host two races. One comes earlier in the season, and one comes later. In 2001, Daytona's track hosted the "Great American Race" in February and a 400-mile race in July. On July 7, Earnhardt, Jr. returned to Daytona.

TRACK FACT
Dale Earnhardt, Jr.'s average speed during his July win at Daytona in 2001 was about 157 mph (253 kph).

The familiar red car had been replaced. Earnhardt, Jr. was driving a white No. 8. It was a tribute car. The tribute was for the 2001 MLB All-Star Game. There was a gray silhouette of a man in full sprint running in front of the rear tire.

It was good old-fashioned racing, however, that propelled Earnhardt, Jr. to victory. After winning, he drove to the grass, climbed out of his car, and stood on the window opening. In his pinstriped white racing suit, he punched his right arm into the sky and let out a yell.

The crowd stood and cheered back. They wanted him to win the race. Michael Waltrip finished second. It was the reverse order of the February race there. But all seemed right with the racing world for that moment.

Earnhardt, Jr.'s next race win was also emotional. It was the first race after the September 11 terrorist attacks in the United States. It was in Dover, Delaware, and it was called the Cal Ripken Jr. 400. Ripken, a famous baseball player, wore number 8 as a player. Many cars were painted with American flags. Earnhardt's car wore one where the trunk would be.

His final win of the season came during the race at Talladega. Talladega is known as a "superspeedway." The average speed during more than three hours of racing was 185.24 miles per hour (298 kilometers per hour).

The track was an Earnhardt favorite. His father had won there the previous year. Sadly, he was not there to see his son carry on the tradition.

Earnhardt, Jr., however, just wanted to win the race. He held first place late in the race, and he was not going to give it up.

With the win, Earnhardt, Jr. moved to sixth in the Cup standings. The rest of the way, however, he would slip. His final position in 2001 was eighth.

That was much better than the sixteenth in his rookie season. Earnhardt, Jr. proved he was no fluke. Under the most trying circumstances, he was a clear success.

The world was taking notice.

DID YOU KNOW?

Dale Earnhardt, Jr. pledged to donate $100 per lap to victims of the September 11 attacks. He completed 400. His donation amounted to $40,000.

THE NEXT STEP

By 2002, Earnhardt, Jr. had met many stars. He dropped some of their names in his book, *Driver #8*, which became a bestseller. Even casual sports fans were interested in his story.

On the track, he had progressed. Off the track, it seemed he had been shot out of a cannon. He splashed into mainstream magazines. He landed on book racks. He appeared on television shows and radio segments.

Often, the connection to his father came up.

As time wore on, Earnhardt, Jr.'s natural talents took over. He had charm. He had appeal. Shifting gears between worlds seemed to come naturally. He had enough southerner in him to pass as a southerner. He had enough interests in him to pass as a modern Renaissance man. He had enough charisma in him to pass as a star.

NASCAR was crossing over. There was once a stereotype about racecar drivers. They were from the South. They had drawls. They were throwbacks to earlier times. They were intolerant. That notion was changing.

Earnhardt, Jr. was among those leading the charge. At first, he was just a kid with a lot of interests. By the turn of the century, his interests were a marketing tool.

In *Driver #8*, Earnhardt, Jr. could go from talking about girls, to cars, to racing, to music, to his niece in a few paragraphs flat. His musical tastes are just as eclectic. He likes some country. He likes some old soul. He likes some rock. And he likes some rap.

In his MTV special, Earnhardt, Jr. is shown bouncing his head to a Nelly song. He has his hat turned backward, and he is driving an SUV.

Earnhardt, Jr. cannot be simply defined.

DID YOU KNOW?

Dale Earnhardt, Jr.'s book, *Driver #8*, spent seventeen weeks on *The New York Times* Best Seller list.

Spectators admire a statue of Earnhardt, Sr., in downtown Kannapolis, North Carolina, after it was unveiled during a ceremony.

BACK TO THE TRACK

Earnhardt, Jr. returned to racing in February 2002. Just before the season, a statue honoring his father was erected at Daytona International Speedway.

To open the season, Earnhardt, Jr. qualified fifth for the Daytona 500. He finished twenty-ninth. Flat tires and an accident pretty much did him in that day.

One nice touch, however, was that he won the Saturday race there. The car was owned by Richard Childress. It was a No. 3 car. The paint scheme and the series were different, but it was still Daytona. And it was still the No. 3, and that made news.

"I know Daddy would be real happy about bringing the No. 3 back to Victory Lane, particularly at Daytona," Earnhardt, Jr. said.[1]

Later that year, he told *Sports Illustrated* that he could feel himself overcoming the loss of his father. "I used to miss him every minute," he said. "Now I've got it down to about every five minutes."[2]

In the next two races, he finished twenty-sixth and sixteenth. It was not until March 10 when he found some satisfaction, finishing second at Atlanta Motor Speedway. The team picked up momentum, finishing fourth the next two contests.

Up next was Texas Motor Speedway on April 8. Earnhardt, Jr. normally ran well there.

Earnhardt, Jr. had moved up to sixth in the standings entering that race. A good finish might mean finding his way to the top five.

Instead, he found adversity.

There were some hints of frustration in previous races. Earnhardt, Jr. preferred to win races. If he did not win, he wanted to finish near the top. When that did not happen, he was not happy.

During that race at Texas in 2002, Earnhardt, Jr. got into an accident. He finished forty-second out of forty-three drivers. He tumbled to eleventh in the standings. "This is real disappointing. We needed to run well here," Earnhardt, Jr. said.[3]

Two solid finishes followed, including a biggie at Talladega. On April 21, he won again there. It marked Earnhardt, Jr.'s second win in a row at the Alabama track.

Afterward, he unselfishly thanked his DEI teammate. Michael Waltrip ran interference for Earnhardt, Jr. near the end of the race.

"It's awfully mentally hard when guys are beating on your bumper and trying to pass you, and you're holding them off so your teammate can win," Earnhardt, Jr. said of Waltrip.[4]

Earnhardt, Jr. moved to fifth in the standings.

"It's just a great win for us," he said. "We're going to try for that championship, and if we keep up like this we'll get it."[5]

The season was looking up again. Then it took a turn for the worst.

SLUMPING

While some expected Earnhardt, Jr. to experience a sophomore slump, it actually happened in his third season. It was between the Talladega races in 2002. After winning on April 21, he found the slump. It would be a long one. And it turned out to be injury-related.

On April 28, Earnhardt, Jr. crashed at a race in Fontana, California. He took a hard hit, one of the hardest of his career. It was reported he suffered a minor bruise to his right ankle. Later in the season, he admitted it was a concussion.

But the points system does not work on sympathy. Earnhardt, Jr. kept racing—even through difficulty. By May 26, he fell to twelfth in points. On August 11, he finished thirty-fifth in a race and fell to seventeenth in points.

Only fourteen races remained that season. It was too late to move very high in points. That did not matter to Earnhardt, Jr. or his team. He continued to race hard.

He probably started feeling better, too. Nine times he finished in the top ten. He closed well down the stretch.

A few days before his twenty-eighth birthday, he put a triumphant end to the slump. On October 6, he

THE SLUMP—2002
Between Talladega Races

Race week	Start	Finish	Laps
10	9	36	225
11	2	36	327
12	6	35	371
13	30	30	396
14	14	12	200
15	3	22	199
16	23	30	109
17	9	6	160
18	9	10	267
19	28	23	300
20	11	37	144
21	3	22	160
22	21	35	84
23	1	10	200
24	2	3	500
25	15	16	367
26	24	4	400
27	37	11	207
28	3	24	396
29	1	6	267

won again at Talladega. That marked his third straight win there. Thanks to a nearly perfect calculation of fuel, his car ran out of gas shortly after he earned the victory.

The rest of the way, he worked toward the top ten. The closest he came was eleventh.

Earnhardt, Jr.'s last race of the season may have summed up 2002. He led a total of forty-six laps, but he wound up finishing twenty-first.

NEW OPPORTUNITIES

Earnhardt, Jr. and Teresa had started a racing company of their own in 2002. They called it Chance2. His mother, Brenda, had also moved back near Mooresville by then.

It also was announced that Earnhardt, Jr. would appear on the cover of a very popular NASCAR video game. The 2003 edition of the game showed Earnhardt, Jr. wearing sunglasses and his red hat backward. By 2003, Earnhardt, Jr. was becoming more focused. Despite all the distractions available to him, his career was gaining more importance to him.

"What was fun as a 21-year-old or a 24-year-old just doesn't have the same impact now," he said. "What means the most to me now is being the best driver in the toughest series in racing."[6]

In part, he pointed to the wreck in California. He even kept a picture of the wreckage. He thought of it as a turning point of his career. He was also more comfortable being called "Junior." It was perfect. It paid tribute to his own successes while still honoring his father.

To open the season, Junior ran well in preliminary races at Daytona. In the 2003 Daytona 500, however, he finished thirty-sixth. But he did lead twenty-two laps. In another bit of good news, DEI teammate Michael Waltrip won his second Daytona 500. A thirty-third-place finish followed for Junior. Then, he took off.

RIDING HIGH

By the fifth race, Earnhardt, Jr. ranked in the top five in points. He would not fall out of it the rest of the season. In fact, he was as high as second.

The first time he saw second was on April 6. He had won at Talladega—again. It marked the fourth time in a row. No one had ever done that before. Not surprisingly, Junior again thrust his right arm into the air and hollered. He had finished second the week before. He finished third the week after.

Clearly, Junior was on a roll. Unlike in 2002, he would not suffer a slump. He did not win another race until the thirty-fourth of thirty-six contests that season. However, he did finish consistently.

His final finish was No. 3 overall. It was his top finish by far. It validated his potential.

He also won twice on the minor-league circuit in a Chance2-owned car. In other words, he owned and drove the car to a win.

In all, Junior won nearly $5 million in official races. He also won NASCAR's Most Popular Driver Award. He had more votes than the next ten drivers combined.

None of this exactly fulfilled him as a driver. He wanted to win the Cup championship.

Even during that season, he looked back at Daytona. He did not like what he saw. Even from his perch in the No. 2 spot at the time.

"At this point in the year, the Daytona 500 is still something that bothers me and bothers the team," he said.[7]

It would make what happened in February 2004 that much more special.

GREATER HIGHS AND LOWS

During the off-season, NASCAR readied to begin its first season with a new sponsor. In a sign of the times, it had moved from a tobacco sponsor to a telecommunications sponsor for 2004.

Many of the racers bridged the gap between old school and new. There were veterans everywhere a fan looked. There were also young guns everywhere, too.

By 2004, Junior was still a blend of old and new school. He was also a veteran on the track. He was nearing thirty years old. It probably surprised him to hear how old he was. At least he now looked his age.

He was no longer an upstart. In fact, in 2001, 2002, and 2003, the Cup champions were all born in the 1970s. At this point, NASCAR racing was a lucrative living. Guys who wanted in entered early. There was enough money in the game to race for great rewards.

As the cars rolled off the starting grid for the 2004 Daytona 500, Junior was a favorite. He wanted to win the race for about a thousand reasons. Some were obvious and public. Some were private but no less obvious.

DID YOU KNOW?

The three drivers who won the points championship in 2001, 2002, and 2003 were born in either 1971 or 1972, and none were southerners.

The date of the race was February 15. It was six years to the day that Earnhardt, Sr. won his Daytona 500.

Junior started the race in the third spot. Rather than red with a white number, his car was mostly white with a red No. 8. The date of the race was stamped on the hood. There was no way Junior would forget it.

Before the race began, he was again asking himself what the media was asking.

"I am my own worst critic," he said. "I used to wonder if I would ever win a Cup race and be able to keep a job driving a racecar. I think I've proven by now that I can. But, in this crazy race—where luck plays such a role—you can't help but wonder if it's just not in the cards for you to win."[1]

THE GREATEST DAY

Not long after the start of the race, Junior revved his way out front. He stayed there for almost thirty laps. Then he raced with the leaders all day. In front of a huge crowd, he turned good lap after good lap in a good car.

Mostly, he raced with Tony Stewart. With twenty laps remaining, he made his move. Junior zipped past the No. 20 in his No. 8. In a personal essay, he described how he set up the pass.

"I tried to pass Tony for seven or eight laps," he said. "I tried every move I knew. Each lap, I tried to do something else to get by, and he did everything to keep me behind him."

"I got a good run, drove my car to the high side, and when Tony went up to block me, I swept back across his bumper and got enough momentum to get a nose out in front. Everything had to be perfect, and I finally got it right."[2]

The two jockeyed for a few tense laps. Junior had made the right move at the right time. Now, he would have to keep running well without being distracted. The turns could not come fast enough.

Junior held on for one of the biggest wins of his career. It was far more important than a car race. "This has got to be the greatest day of my life," he said from Victory Lane.[3]

Not surprisingly, his thoughts quickly turned to his father. His father and the Daytona 500 were like the Red Sox and the World Series. For the longest time, there were spectacular losses—then tremendous victory.

Junior only had to wait five years. He wanted to win just as badly each time.

"I'm not ashamed to say I put a lot of emphasis on coming down here and winning this race just because of what I've been through down here. You see Dad run second, blow tires out, flip over on the back straightaway year after year after year after year," Earnhardt, Jr. said. "Inside of me, back then, just a little bit of wanting to win this race started up, and it's been building ever since."[4]

Junior soaked in the win. He was champion of the Daytona 500. "The weight of the world had been

TRACK FACT

Dale Earnhardt, Jr. held Tony Stewart off down the stretch of the Daytona 500 and won by .273 seconds.

Earnhardt, Jr. celebrates his 2004 Daytona 500 victory.

lifted off my shoulders," he said, "and everything sort of went into slow motion."[5]

Rather than go straight to Victory Lane, Junior pried his body free of the cockpit and sat on the windowsill of his car. He threw a left fist into the air and saluted the fans.

The reality finally began to hit him.

"I'm a Daytona 500 champion," he said. "I can't believe it."[6]

The win was significant for a couple of reasons. Junior added to the family resume at Daytona. He also accepted comparisons to his father. It showed a man comfortable in his own skin.

"I feel you can compare me to him today because we've done so much over the last three years here," he said. "I just want to keep adding to what he did."[7]

Of course, as much effort as the 500 takes, there is a whole season that follows. It is grueling. In fact, Junior needed to return to the track to race again the following day. The race that is usually held the day before the Daytona 500 was interrupted by rain thirty-one laps into the scheduled 120. It had to be finished on Monday. Junior won that race, too. He was well on his way in 2004.

Earnhardt, Jr. acknowledges the crowd as he parks his car on the finish line after winning the Daytona 500.

A FRIGHTENING CRASH

Junior suffered only one early setback that season. He was rarely outside of the top ten. By the fourth week of the season, he was in third and did not spend a day out of the top five the rest of the way. He even spent seven consecutive weeks in the points lead.

Unfortunately, an on-track incident proved the biggest scare of Junior's career. He also felt his father's hand in that incident. Junior had a terrible crash in July. It was during a warm-up for an American Le Mans Series race in California. It was not a typical crash against the wall. The way the car hit, gasoline spilled into the car and set off a huge fire in the cockpit.

Flames were shooting around him. Junior had to escape, but he was a little shaken up and strapped into the cockpit. Time was running out. He had to flee the inferno.

Junior regained his senses enough to pull himself out of the car.

Later, he would say that he felt his father's presence. It might have saved him from a catastrophe.

Before getting out, Junior was badly burned on his neck and legs. During the next few weeks, he could start Cup races, but he could not finish them.

Earnhardt, Jr. talks about the burns he suffered after a crash.

A LITTLE HELP FROM HIS FRIENDS

With the help of other drivers relieving him in the No. 8, Junior did not lose ground. By November, he was still in the running. He stood in second. Unfortunately, he went for a win that weekend in Georgia and wound up crashing.

The No. 8 limped to a thirty-third-place finish with its nose pushed nearly to the windshield. Junior admitted he was racing to win. The points leaders had trouble that day. Junior wanted to gain ground. Instead, he fell to fifth in the standings.

It was a flash of the old Junior. He wanted to win the race. Even if it cost him, he took his shot. Sometimes, that pays off. Other times, it does not.

It may not have been exactly the way he wanted things to go, but he did win a career-high six races in the 2004 season, including another race at Talladega. He set a number of career highs, scoring thirteen top-three finishes, sixteen top-five finishes, and winning more prize money than he ever had before.

For the second year in a row, he won the Most Popular Driver Award, too.

In addition, the team he owned in the minor leagues won a title in that division. His driver was Martin Truex Jr.

Junior had raced to strong and not-so-strong season finishes (sixteenth, eighth, eleventh, third, and fifth). As 2005 approached, changes also approached. Those changes would test Junior's spirits again.

TOUGH CHANGES

There was a shakeup in the off-season. It was decided that most of the No. 8 crew would work with another DEI racing crew. Junior's cousin, Eury, Jr., would not be part of the operation.

The race team suffered. Junior opened the season with a third-place finish at Daytona. Then things took a bad turn.

Within three races, he was twenty-seventh in points. The team tried to pull things together, but the season ended in disappointment. Junior finished nineteenth in the standings. He won only one race. As a season, it was his poorest statistically.

Because of a new points system, Junior knew his season was over by the twenty-sixth of thirty-six races. In the new format, which started in 2004, teams compete to the twenty-sixth race, and only the top ten drivers at that point race for the title. It is called the Chase for the Cup.

Even though Junior was out of it, Eury, Jr. was brought

TRACK FACT
Dale Earnhardt, Jr.'s career-high six wins in 2004 came at Daytona, Atlanta, Richmond, Bristol, Talladega, and Phoenix.

back to be his crew chief. Their relationship, like those in many families, could get strained. When millions of dollars are on the line and when one guy's mostly responsible for the car the other is driving, things become complicated.

DID YOU KNOW?

Dale Earnhardt, Jr. placed in the top five only seven times in 2005, compared to thirteen finishes of thirty or lower.

"It's all family," Earnhardt, Jr. said. "Sometimes it's better, and sometimes it's not, but I think most of the time all of us being family is a good thing."[8]

Toward the end of 2004, all the pressures to win hurt their working relationship. That even hurt their personal relationship. But the adversity of 2005 made them rethink their differences.

By 2006, they were ready to carry on.

STILL RUNNING IN HIGH GEAR

Even before 2006 dawned, Junior was looking forward to it. He had won a third consecutive Most Popular Driver Award in 2005. His racecar in the minors won a second consecutive championship. He and his cousin had been reunited.

After four races, Junior had two top-ten finishes. At that point, he ranked seventh in the standings.

He also showed something special at the spring race at Talladega on May 1. The red No. 8 was nowhere to be seen. Instead, he drove a black

Earnhardt, Jr. (8) practices at Talladega Superspeedway.

No. 8 car. It wore Junior's sponsors and markings, but it was a tribute car. It was made to look like his father's No. 3.

The race was set for April 30, but it was postponed by rain. The previous Saturday would have been Earnhardt, Sr.'s fifty-fifth birthday. Junior finished thirty-first.

A week later, he won a race. It was his first trip to Victory Lane in nearly a year. He started the race tenth. By the sixtieth lap, he had worked his way to the top eight. From there, he pulled the car into the top three for almost the rest of the way. Then he took the lead and held on for his first win since the previous

July. His winless streak had lasted twenty-seven races. The win confirmed what race fans were thinking. Junior was back—at least for a time.

A ROUGH PATCH

The next week, Junior felt ill for a race in Darlington, South Carolina. He managed to run all 500 miles. He finished fifth. A backup driver was not necessary. Driver No. 8 wanted to finish the race.

During the next seven races, he shot up to third in the points race. That summer, the animated movie *Cars* was released. It featured Junior's voice. While that may have been a highlight for him, the rest of the summer proved difficult.

The racing season is a long one. Junior hit a summer skid. The worst of it came in the nineteenth and twentieth races of the season. In each, he finished last.

On July 16, he blew an engine at New Hampshire. On July 23, he wound up in an accident at Pocono. His car had to be hauled off by a tow truck. In previous seasons, Junior and Eury, Jr. might have clashed over something like this. Rather than lash out at each other, the cousins backed off.

"I'm going to enjoy my week [off] at the beach," Eury, Jr. said after the crash. "[Junior's] going to enjoy his week in Las Vegas. You've got to take it and go on."[1]

Earnhardt, Jr. arrives with family and friends for the movie _Cars_ at Lowe's Motor Speedway in Concord, North Carolina, on May 26, 2006.

Eury, Jr. explained how the cousins were maturing. They knew they still had a great chance to make the Chase.

"Last year, that team was pretty down on itself halfway through the year," he said. "We've got something to prove, and I think we showed it all year [so far]."[2]

After the back-to-back last-place finishes, Junior raced at the Brickyard in Indianapolis Motor Speedway.

A *New York Times* writer called the race "the second-most prestigious on the Nextel Cup schedule, behind only the Daytona 500." That story's title was "Time Is Not On Earnhardt's Side."[3]

But optimism sure was.

"I really wanted to get right back to the racetrack—especially after the bad finish we had at Pocono," Junior said.[4]

A good finish followed at the Brickyard. He placed sixth there on August 6. At the next race, he finished eighteenth.

Then he made a run.

CHALLENGING FOR THE TITLE

As he might on the track, Earnhardt, Jr. kept moving up the pack in the points race. First, he earned a sixth-place finish at Michigan on August 20. Next, it was a third at Bristol on August 26. Then it was a second at California on September 3.

That run assured him a spot in the Chase. The Chase races began on September 17 and ran through November 19. In Junior's ten Chase races, he finished as high as third and as low as twenty-third.

The twenty-third-place finish on October 8 was tough to swallow. The twenty-second-place finish at Martinsville might have been worse. On October 8, he was leading at Talladega, again, and was spun from the race on the final lap.

On October 22, he had only five more races in the season. He would have to make up ground in the Chase. He stood sixth in the points.

Maybe the twenty-third-place finish was still in his head. Maybe he just wanted to win a race. Having turned thirty-two earlier in the month, he still had not fully outgrown the urge to win races without calculating the potential cost if he failed.

But who could blame him? That is what he does for a living—racing to win. Unfortunately, it cost him at Martinsville. With less than twenty-five laps remaining, Junior tried to make a move he probably should not have. He crashed.

"I was just trying to finish in the top five instead of just driving a little smarter," he said after the race. "I just wasn't smart. There's no excuse.

"I've got to learn how to have a little more patience."[5]

Junior slipped to sixth in the points standings. A higher finish would likely have placed him close to the driver's seat in the top of the standings. Instead, the new points leader was old friend Matt Kenseth.

"I'm just disappointed because we had an opportunity," Junior said. "With only four races [left], I don't know, anything's possible. I could just be in so much a better situation right now."[6]

The race winner that day was Jimmie Johnson, who moved up four places to third in the points race. After the race, Junior was down. He told *Sports Illustrated* as much the next day. Two of his closest team members, including Eury, Jr., came to his office. They told him they would not trade their situation for anyone's.

"You're our guy," they told him.[7]

Earnhardt, Jr. finished third in the next race, which was October 29. He was in fourth in the standings. Kenseth remained in first. Johnson moved up to second.

On November 5, Junior was still in the hunt, but he was sick. He battled flu symptoms to finish sixth. His car also hit the wall in that race. His finish after those circumstances was impressive. After the race, he thanked his team.

"It would be great to be called resilient," he said. "This team is really strong, very dedicated. They have carried me whenever I needed it. We're putting up a great fight. I don't think anybody anticipated this team running this strong every week. I'm proud of my team."[8]

Johnson moved into the first spot in the Chase. Kenseth was second.

In the next race on November 12, Junior's hopes pretty much came to an end. Johnson finished second at Phoenix. Junior finished ninth.

Junior dropped two places to fifth in the points race, and Johnson held onto first. That is just how the season ended after Junior's nineteenth-place finish in the season finale.

"I can't express how proud I am of this team. I just have a tremendous team behind me," Earnhardt said afterward. "They just never gave up all year. We battled back when we are down race after race. We battled back today.

"We made the Chase, and we fought hard, and we are going to try and do that next year [because] we have a great team—just a really, really great team."[9]

His fifth-place standing made it three of four years in that company. And again he earned the Most Popular Driver Award.

"I can't tell you how far we've come since 2005," he told *Sports Illustrated* before the 2007 season.[10]

DID YOU KNOW?

Dale Earnhardt, Jr. has appeared on more than 100 magazine covers.

A SEASON OF CHALLENGES

The 2007 season brought changes both on and off the track. After starting the season with two bad races, Earnhardt, Jr. found himself in fortieth place in the point standings. By the season's midpoint, he had climbed to twelfth place in the standings, but he would get no higher. After 26 races, he stood in thirteenth place, just one spot away from a place in the Chase for the Nextel Cup. He finished the season

Earnhardt, Jr. poses with the new car he will be driving for Hendrick Motorsports.

in sixteenth place, and for the first time in his career, he did not win a race.

Off the track, Earnhardt, Jr. once again found himself the center point of one of the biggest NASCAR stories of the season. Since he began his career, he had raced for Dale Earnhardt Inc. (DEI), the company founded by his late father and now run by his stepmother, Teresa Earnhardt. With his contract set to expire at the end of the 2007 racing season, Earnhardt had been in negotiations all year to take majority ownership of DEI. When that effort failed, Earnhardt, Jr. announced that he was leaving Dale Earnhardt Inc.

Only five weeks after leaving his family's venture at DEI, Earnhardt, Jr. had signed a five-year contract to join racing's most elite team: Hendrick Motorsports. He left behind the No. 8 car and announced that he would drive car No. 88 instead. To top it off, Hendrick later signed Tony Eury, Jr. to a two-year deal to join the team as Earnhardt, Jr.'s crew chief.

MATURING INTO HIS ROLE

Earnhardt, Jr. has come a long way in his life—both professionally and personally. He dreamed of racing as a kid and worked hard to make that dream come true. Then he was a racecar driver while he was still trying to grow up.

Somewhere along the way he became a man and a racecar driver. By the time he hit thirty years old, he had known fame for more than half his life. Sometimes he courted it. Other times he shunned it. As an adult, he seems to accept it.

"At 32, he has matured and grown into his starring role," *The New York Times'* Selena Roberts wrote in 2006.[11]

For the rest of his racing career, however long it lasts, he will be considered a veteran.

Something else had been happening in NASCAR racing. Over the years, there were bigger teams and bigger racing programs competing. In some races, his car entered as an underdog. His NASCAR points title hopes have even been questioned.

Dale Earnhardt, Jr. is part owner of a motorsports entertainment complex near Mobile, Alabama.

"I'll be the first to admit that we had a lot more exposure over the last five or six years given to us that's sort of out of line compared to what we've won and how we've run," he said in 2006.[12]

It is because his story is undeniably interesting.

He is the son of a tough father who became famous for being a tough legend in a tough sport. Junior may have had it easier in some ways because of his father, but Junior certainly did not have anything handed to him.

At one point, he was just a kid who was chased by flames from a burning house. At another, he was just someone getting to really know his father when he was lost in a car accident.

By his thirties, Junior was an adult with a wildly successful career of his own. He had won millions of dollars. He had earned millions more in sponsorships. In addition, Junior has raised tens of thousands of dollars for charity.

He made a splash as a driver in a music video with Jay-Z. The rapper had retired from the music industry briefly. He was making a comeback. In the video, Jay-Z is riding shotgun to Junior.

As he circles tracks, Junior is also more aware of the big picture in his races. Having already surpassed

Junior carries the Olympic torch down Brevard Street in Charlotte, North Carolina, on December 5, 2001.

his father's fortune with more than $41 million in career earnings, the change to stock car racing's most elite team could bring Earnhardt, Jr. to even more unforeseen plateaus.

NASCAR, meanwhile, is forging ahead on the momentum of its lucrative recent past. The circuit is entering yet another of its own phases. A "Car of Tomorrow" debuted in 2007, primarily to increase safety in the wake of the death of Earnhardt, Sr. Hendrick Motorsports drivers have dominated the races in which the Car of Tomorrow has been used.

Maybe the future will be found in the most present version of its storied past: Dale Earnhardt, Jr.

CAREER STATISTICS

Year	Rank	Starts	Wins	Poles
2007	16	36	0	1
2006	5	36	1	0
2005	19	36	1	0
2004	5	36	6	0
2003	3	36	2	0
2002	11	36	2	2
2001	8	36	3	2
2000	16	34	2	2
1999	48	5	0	0

Top 5	Top 10	Earnings	Points
7	12	$5,221,970	3,929
10	17	$5,466,100	6,328
7	13	$5,761,830	3,780
16	21	$7,201,380	6,368
13	21	$4,923,500	4,815
11	16	$4,570,980	4,270
9	15	$5,384,630	4,460
3	5	$2,610,400	3,516
0	1	$162,095	500

CAREER ACHIEVEMENTS

- Earned the Most Popular Driver Award for the fourth consecutive season in 2006.

- Two-time champion (1998, 1999) in NASCAR's top minor league.

- Became the first third-generation champion of a NASCAR division.

- Tied Davey Allison and Jimmie Johnson by winning his second race in NASCAR's top division in only his sixteenth start.

- Set two track records in his first full season (Charlotte and Michigan) in the top division.

- Set a record by winning four consecutive races at Talladega Motor Speedway from 2001 through 2003.

- In 2004, became a championship owner when Martin Truex Jr. won a title in NASCAR's top minor league with a car owned by Chance2.

- Co-owns Chance2 with his stepmother, Teresa Earnhardt.

- Owns JR Motorsports, which fields a team in NASCAR's top minor league.

CHAPTER NOTES

CHAPTER 1. THE WORST TURN

1. "Dream a little dream," Ticker, February 6, 2001, <http://sportsillustrated.cnn.com/motorsports/2001/daytona500/news/2001/02/06/nascar_earnhardt_junior/>.

2. "Dale Earnhardt, through his son's eyes," *nascar.com*, October 18, 2000, <http://www.usatoday.com/sports/motor/earnhardt/2001-02-22-earnhardtjr.htm>.

3. Ibid.

4. "The Last Lap," *Sports Illustrated*, March 5, 2001.

5. Dale Earnhardt, Jr. with Jade Gurss, *Driver #8*, Warner Vision Books, 2002, p. 348.

6. "Earnhardt, Jr. will race Sunday," *espn.com*, February 20, 2001, <http://espn.go.com/rpm/wc/2001/0220/1097157.html>.

CHAPTER 2. THE EARLY YEARS

1. Bob Knotts, "One driven family," usaweekend.com, August. 28-30, 1998, <http://www.usaweekend.com/98_issues/980830/980830earnhardt.html>.

2. Larry Cothren and the Editors of *Stock Car Racing Magazine*, *Dale Earnhardt, Jr.: Making a Legend of His Own*, St. Paul, Minn.: MBI Publishing Company, 2005, p. 7.

3. Carrie Seidman, "Youthful Earnhardt Racing Ahead of the Good Old Boys," *New York Times*, August 4, 1980.

4. Ibid.

5. David Poole, "Difficult? Kelley and Jr. have been there before," *thatsracin.com*, July 9, 2006, <http://www.thatsracin.com/mld/thatsracin/14996706.htm>.

6. Scott Fowler, "Little E has a lot to say," charlotte.com, May 20, 2006, <http://www.charlotte.com/mld/charlotte/sports/columnists/scott_fowler/14625977.htm>.

7. David Poole, "Difficult? Kelley and Jr. have been there before," *thatsracin.com*, July 9, 2006, <http://www.thatsracin.com/mld/thatsracin/14996706.htm>.

8. Scott Fowler, "Little E has a lot to say," *charlotte.com*, May 20, 2006, <http://www.charlotte.com/mld/charlotte/sports/columnists/scott_fowler/14625977.htm>.

9.   Scoop Malinowski, "The Biofiles: Dale Earnhardt, Jr.," *cbs. sportsline.com*, February 14, 2006, <http://cbs.sportsline.com/ spinstory/9233702>.

CHAPTER 3. RACING DAYS

1.   Terrence Cheromcka, "Who-Files," *timeforkids.com*, June 18, 2002, <http://www.timeforkids.com/TFK/specials/story/0,6079,263484,00. html>.
2.   "Lean on me," *sportsillustrated.com*, February 1, 2003, <http:// sportsillustrated.cnn.com/motorsports/nascar_plus/news/2003/02/01/ earnhardt_sister_ap/>.
3.   Dale Earnhardt, Jr., "Military school helped me grow up," *nascar. com*, August 30, 2001, <http://www.nascar.com/2001/NEWS/08/29/ dalejr_column/index.html>.
4.   Ibid.
5.   Joanne Korth, "Family tradition drives 'other son' forward," *sptimes.com*, June 18, 2002, <http://www.sptimes.com/2002/06/30/ Sports/Family_tradition_driv.shtml>.
6.   Darrell Waltrip, "I don't want to ever forget," *msn.foxsports. com*, 2001, <http://msn.foxsports.com/other/story/7879>.
7.   Ibid.

CHAPTER 4. SHOWING PROMISE

1.   Michael Vega, "Changing gears," *Boston Globe*, February 15, 2004.
2.   Dale Earnhardt, Jr. with Jade Gurss, *Driver #8*, Warner Vision Books, 2002, p. 42.
3.   Larry Cothren and the Editors of *Stock Car Racing Magazine*, *Dale Earnhardt, Jr.: Making a Legend of His Own*, St. Paul, Minn.: MBI Publishing Company, 2005, p. 43.
4.   The Earnhardts, *nascar.com*, <http://www.nascar.com/2002/ kyn/families/02/01/earnhardts/>.

CHAPTER 5. SATURDAY SPECIAL

1.   Dale Earnhardt, Jr. with Jade Gurss, *Driver #8*, Warner Vision Books, 2002, p. 46.

2.   Larry Cothren and the Editors of *Stock Car Racing Magazine*, *Dale Earnhardt, Jr.: Making a Legend of His Own*, St. Paul, Minn.: MBI Publishing Company, 2005, p. 54.

3.   Dale Earnhardt, Jr. with Jade Gurss, *Driver #8*, Warner Vision Books, 2002, p. 47.

4.   Loren Mooney, "The Son Also Rises," *Sports Illustrated*, June 1, 1998.

5.   Dale Earnhardt, Jr. with Jade Gurss, *Driver #8*, Warner Vision Books, 2002, p. 4.

6.   Tarik El-Bashir, "Never on Sunday, Until Now for Earnhardt," *New York Times*, February 16, 1998.

7.   "Penny for his thoughts?," *sportsillustrated.com*, July 6, 1998, <http://sportsillustrated.cnn.com/motorsports/events/1998/daytona/news/1998/07/06/earnhardtpenny_update/>.

8.   Larry Cothren and the Editors of *Stock Car Racing Magazine*, *Dale Earnhardt, Jr.: Making a Legend of His Own*, St. Paul, Minn.: MBI Publishing Company, 2005, p. 30.

CHAPTER 6. SUNDAY SCHOOL

1.   Jeff MacGregor, "Dale Earnhardt, Jr. and NASCAR Nation," *Sports Illustrated,* July 1, 2002.

2.   Dale Earnhardt, Jr. with Jade Gurss, *Driver #8*, Warner Vision Books, 2002, p. 51.

3.   Larry Woody, "Here's looking at you kid," *Nashville Tennessean*, May 30, 1999.

4.   Larry Cothren and the Editors of *Stock Car Racing Magazine*, *Dale Earnhardt, Jr.: Making a Legend of His Own*, St. Paul, Minn.: MBI Publishing Company, 2005, p. 59.

5.   Ibid., p. 66.

6.   Larry Woody, "Junior's success due to hard work, not last name," *Nashville Tennessean*, June 1, 2003.

7.   Dale Earnhardt, Jr. with Jade Gurss, *Driver #8*, Warner Vision Books, 2002, p. xxiii.

8.   Skip Wood, "Earnhardt, Jr. returns to site of first win," *usatoday.com*, March 29, 2001, <http://www.usatoday.com/sports/motor/nascar/2001-03-29-earnhardt-jr.htm>.

9.   Dale Earnhardt, Jr. with Jade Gurss, *Driver #8*, Warner Vision Books, 2002, p. 102.

10. Dale Earnhardt, Jr. with Jade Gurss, *Driver #8*, Warner Vision Books, 2002, p. 105.

11. Ibid., p. 146-147.

CHAPTER 7. BITTERSWEET VICTORY

1.   "Dale Earnhardt, through his son's eyes," *nascar.com*, Oct. 18, 2000, <http://www.usatoday.com/sports/motor/earnhardt/2001-02-22-earnhardtjr.htm>.

2.   Dale Earnhardt, Jr. with Jade Gurss, *Driver #8*, Warner Vision Books, 2002, p. 311.

3.   Ibid., p. 343.

4.   "Earnhardt, Jr. will race Sunday," *espn.com*, Feb. 20, 2001, < http://espn.go.com/rpm/wc/2001/0220/1097157.html>.

5.   Darrell Waltrip, "What would Dad do?," *msn.foxsports.com*, 2001, <http://msn.foxsports.com/story/7878>.

6.   Ibid.

7.   Dave Caldwell, "Quietly, Earnhardt, Jr. Focuses on His Racing," *New York Times*, April 22, 2001.

CHAPTER 8. THE NEXT STEP

1.   Marty Smith, "Earnhardt, Jr., Waltrip: Potent 1-2 punch," *nascar.com*, April 21, 2002, <http://www.nascar.com/2002/news/headlines/bg/02/16/daytona_opener/index.html>.

2.   Jeff MacGregor, "Dale Earnhardt, Jr. and NASCAR Nation," *Sports Illustrated*, July 1, 2002.

3.   Dave Rodman, "Cars of Dale Jr., Burton take a beating at Texas," *nascar.com*, April 8, 2002, <http://www.nascar.com/2002/news/headlines/wc/04/08/jr_texas/index.html>.

4.   Marty Smith, "Earnhardt, Jr., Waltrip: Potent 1-2 punch," *nascar.com*, April 21, 2002, <http://www.nascar.com/2002/news/headlines/wc/04/21/dei_dega/index.html>.

5.   Dave Rodman, "Cars of Dale Jr., Burton take a beating at Texas," *nascar.com*, April 22, 2002, <http://www.nascar.com/2002/news/headlines/wc/04/21/cup_lead/index.html>.

6.   Larry Cothren and the Editors of *Stock Car Racing Magazine*, *Dale Earnhardt, Jr.: Making a Legend of His Own*, St. Paul, Minn.: MBI Publishing Company, 2005, p. 143.

7.   Larry Cothren and the Editors of *Stock Car Racing Magazine*, *Dale Earnhardt, Jr.: Making a Legend of His Own*, St. Paul, Minn.: MBI Publishing Company, 2005, p. 144.

CHAPTER 9. GREATER HIGHS AND LOWS

1.   Larry Cothren and the Editors of *Stock Car Racing Magazine*, *Dale Earnhardt, Jr.: Making a Legend of His Own*, St. Paul, Minn.: MBI Publishing Company, 2005, p. 174.

2.   Ibid., p. 179.

3.   Viv Bernstein, "Father's Legacy Inspires Earnhardt, Jr.," *New York Times*, February 16, 2004.

4.   Ibid.

5.   Larry Cothren and the Editors of *Stock Car Racing Magazine*, *Dale Earnhardt, Jr.: Making a Legend of His Own*, St. Paul, Minn.: MBI Publishing Company, 2005, p. 180.

6.   Viv Bernstein, "Father's Legacy Inspires Earnhardt, Jr.," *New York Times*, February 16, 2004.

7.   "Earnhardt ends Daytona run with Busch victory," *sportsillustrated.com*, February 16, 2004, <http://sportsillustrated.cnn.com/2004/racing/specials/daytona500/2004/02/16/bc.car.nascar.busch.ap/index.html>.

8.   Larry Cothren and the Editors of *Stock Car Racing Magazine*, *Dale Earnhardt, Jr.: Making a Legend of His Own*, St. Paul, Minn.: MBI Publishing Company, 2005, p. 160.

CHAPTER 10. STILL RUNNING IN HIGH GEAR

1.   David Newton, "Earnhardt, Jr., team not stressed over standings," *nascar.com*, July 24, 2006, <http://www.nascar.com/2006/news/headlines/cup/07/23/dearnhardtjr_pocono/index.html>.

2.   Ibid.

3.   Dave Caldwell, "Time Is Not On Earnhardt's Side," *New York Times*, August 6, 2006.

4.   Ibid.

5.   David Newton, "Junior admits need for patience in points race," *nascar.com*, October 23, 2006, <http://www.nascar.com/2006/news/headlines/cup/10/22/dearnhardtjr.points.martinsville/index.html>.

6.   Ibid.

7.   Lars Anderson, "Prime Time For Junior," *Sports Illustrated Presents: NASCAR Preview '07*, December 12, 2006.

8.   David Newton, "Sickness, wall can't keep Junior out of Chase hunt," *nascar.com*, November 6, 2006, <http://www.nascar.com/2006/news/headlines/cup/11/05/dearnhardtjr.texas/index.html>.

9.   Dave Rodman, "Hamlin, Junior go down battling at Homestead," *nascar.com*, November 20, 2006, <http://www.nascar.com/2006/news/headlines/cup/11/20/dhamlin_dearnhardtjr/index.html>.

10. Lars Anderson, "Prime Time For Junior," *Sports Illustrated Presents: NASCAR Preview '07,* December 12, 2006.

11. Selena Roberts, "Nascar Hits Bump On Way to Johnson's Title," *New York Times*, November 20, 2006.

12. "With Victory, Earnhardt's Competence Matches Confidence," *New York Times*, May 8, 2006.

FOR MORE INFORMATION

ON THE WEB

Dale Earnhardt, Jr.'s official Web page: http://www.dalejr.com/

Dale Earnhardt, Jr.'s nascar.com Web page:
http://www.nascar.com/drivers/dps/dearnhar01/cup/index.html

JR Motorsports official Web page: http://www.jrmotorsport.com/

FURTHER READING

Cothren, Larry and the Editors of *Stock Car Racing Magazine*. *Dale Earnhardt, Jr.: Making a Legend of His Own*. St. Paul, Minn.: MBI Publishing Company, 2005.

Earnhardt, Dale Jr. with Jade Gurss. *Driver #8*. New York: Warner Books, 2002.

Montville, Lee. *At the Altar of Speed: The Fast Life and Tragic Death of Dale Earnhardt*. New York: Doubleday, 2001.

GLOSSARY

banking—The sloping of a racetrack, particularly at a curve or a corner, from the apron to the outside wall.

chassis—The combination of a car's floorboard, interior, and roll cage.

draft—The aerodynamic effect that allows two or more cars traveling nose to tail to run faster than a single car.

drafting—The practice of two or more cars, while racing, to run nose to tail, almost touching.

fabricator—A person who specializes in creating the sheet metal body of a stock car. Most teams employ two or more fabricators.

handling—Generally, a racecar's performance while racing, qualifying, or practicing. How a car handles is determined by its tires, suspension geometry, aerodynamics, and other factors.

loose—A condition created when the back end of the vehicle wants to overtake the front end when it is either entering or exiting a turn.

pit road—The area where pit crews service the cars. Generally located along the front straightaway, but because of space limitations, some racetracks sport pit roads on the front and back straightaways.

pit stall—The area along pit road that is designated for a particular team's use during pit stops. Each car stops in the team's stall before being serviced.

pole position—Slang term for the foremost position on the starting grid, awarded to the fastest qualifier.

push—A condition that occurs when the front tires of a vehicle will not turn crisply in a corner.

restrictor plate—An aluminum plate designed to reduce the flow of air and fuel into the engine's combustion chamber, thereby decreasing horsepower and speed.

setup—Slang term for the tuning and adjustments made to a racecar's suspension before and during a race.

short track—Racetracks that are less than one mile in length.

superspeedway—A racetrack of one mile or more in distance.

Victory Lane—Sometimes called the winner's circle. The spot on each racetrack's infield where the race winner parks for the celebration.

INDEX